DEDICATION

To the millennials

"Invest in yourself and work hard when your young, so that you can retire and escape the rat race earlier"

ACKNOWLEDGEMENTS

Would like to thank my father, without whom I wouldn't have understood the importance of having assets which pay your expenses, instead of the general consensus that only income can be used to pay expenses. Thank you Krish, Priyanka and Jehan for helping me polish this offering to all the millennials worldwide.

TABLE OF CONTENTS

1. FINANCIAL FREEDOM: WHAT IT IS AND WHAT IT ENTAILS
2. FINANCIAL INTELLIGENCE
3. STUDYING FINANCIAL STATEMENTS
4. THE INVESTMENT PHILOSOPHY
5. CREATING MORE INCOME
6. WHY IS FINANCIAL FREEDOM EASIER NOW, THAN EVER
7. HOW DO I START TODAY?
8. NETWORKING – THE UNDERRATED WEALTH CREATOR
9. CHANGE YOUR MENTAL ATTITUDE TOWARDS PERSONAL FINANCE
10. REVERSE ENGINEER TO SQUARE ONE
11. BE DRIVEN, BUT BE CAUTIOUS
12. EVERY FAILURE IS A STEP CLOSER TO SUCCESS
13. COVID INVESTING
14. CONCLUSION

FINANCIAL FREEDOM: WHAT IT IS AND WHAT IT ENTAILS

While the textbook definition of 'Financial freedom' encompasses an individual having enough savings, investments, and cash on hand to afford a reasonable lifestyle, he wants for himself and his family without having to rely on formal employment. However, in today's time and age where 'instant gratification' is king and how one defines a reasonable lifestyle dynamically evolves, 'Financial Freedom' has become that much more crucial to understand and thrive toward. When an individual is financially free, typically it means that he is under no scrutiny by creditors, in a nutshell he/she is free of financial liable. Cash is king, having a high disposable income and/or a strong bank balance, always gives you liquidity be it for safety and emergencies.

Every individual should aim for financial freedom, as it brings about an inherent independence which while intangible is nevertheless very precious. It is a way for your mind to get attuned to the responsible version of yourself, there is real growth in one's personality once you are on the way towards financial independence. When you become financially independent, you are more responsible in decision making, since you have already withstood numerous ups and downs, the experience gained is invaluable. A fancy Ivy League MBA would also pale in comparison.

Experience is nothing but the journey of failure and immense amount of decision making under pressure and with difficult choices involved. Your future lies in your hands.

Experience with handling of money responsibly is very rewarding, if one can make mistakes earlier and learn from these mistakes. When you fail earlier on in your life, your postmillennial age is much more rich in wealth and in experience. Giving you the ammunition to spring ahead like an arrow in your journey towards financial freedom, rather than inhibit the individual from growing financially. Each example takes a relative scenario, as the target audience can be varied, one can look to relate to it, if not with 100% accuracy.

Just as there are stages and milestones in any long and trying path, financial freedom broadly has six stages. I believe the first step starts with creating a budget, so one cannot be lagging on payment of liabilities and never miss out on their investment commitments. This stage will also include measures of taking care of yourself, paying rent, electricity, telephone, and whatever other expense incurred to ensure basic standard of living. The second or the next stage, would be maintaining liquidity for 6 months of expenses, to avoid dropping the minimum standard of living in case of an adverse scenario (job loss, earthquake, pandemic like COVID-19). Most of us millennials will not be able to do that or are not currently able to do that. Perhaps the 'You Only Live Once' mentality adopted to explain away large discretionary expenses is one big hurdle in our way during this stage. The third stage is more foresight driven, once you have levelled up in life you should not be content, the previous savings goals should be revised to include the additional income that you are earning, for example from six months of maintenance of expenditure the goal should now be a year's expenditure. Not only does this make us more conscious about our spending decisions but also allows for security, flexibility, and a form of insurance if there is a decision to change the current way of living or in other words pursue desires without looking back. The fourth stage would be looking to take up investing in stocks, real estate or even enterprising, this will require doubling the savings mentioned in the previous stage, as a safety basket. This is where aside from using your current money responsibly, there is also a need to self-educate and create your Financial IQ, in depth about asset classes, reasonable expected ROIs and diversifications. This stage allows you to take on new risks, mainly because you have a safety fund. When you accomplish this stage of freedom, personally you should have a sense of accomplishment, because of the experiences that has shaped you to come this far and gear towards the next stages of financial freedom. The next and probably a level only a handful people in your own network might have surpassed is the fifth level, where you have enough savings for yourself for lifetime (up to the age of 75 i.e. average living age). One can do this by saving a large amount and living off the interest of that or the other option would be to own income producing assets which allow freedom to pursue other endeavours and have a lifetime of financial freedom. The last and final (sixth) stage is wealth aplenty, where wealth is more than one can spend in a lifetime, this allows for philanthropic endeavours such as donations in foundations for the betterment of society, college funds for children ready when they are at school, money for future generations and many other self-actualisation goals. As you scale up to levels of financial freedom in life, the options of location, hobbies, interests, and entrepreneurship endeavours will increase in life, this has a negative correlation with the financial stress in life.

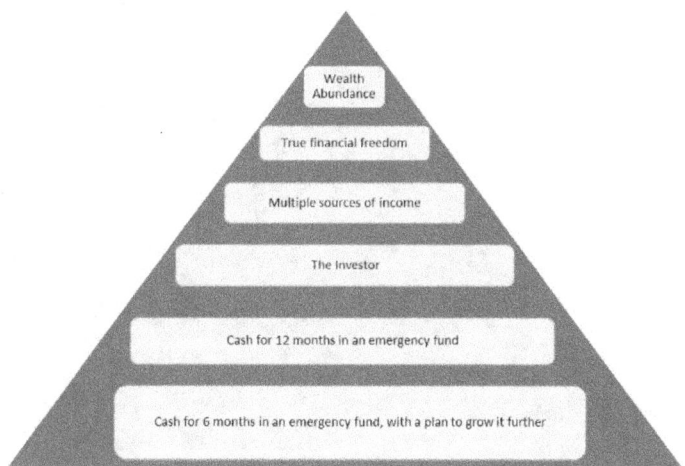

Power of Compounding- Is also known as the 8th wonder of the world. Why? Because it can grow the principal into a multi-bagger. When you invest in yourself, the knowledge, skills and experience you acquire earlier, can help you become financially independent, even faster, and richer i.e. both in experience and in wealth.

What does financial freedom do for you?

1. Financial plan - Gives you assessment about how to deal with future cashflows (both inward and outward)
2. Allows you to invest in endeavours i.e. financial and non-financially driven
3. Success percentage increases over time
4. Goal based investing, allows finance to be the last reason for not pursuing your goals
5. Attention is paid for the future
6. Buys the real and finite asset- Time
7. Increases capacity to take responsibility and an action plan
8. one's bandwidth to pursue other interests read and study
9. Solution oriented
10. Make time for family another loved ones

We are all are capable of being financially independent, we need to get over patterns that we are mentally stuck to. To be financially independent, you must be financially intelligent; one must grow their Financial IQ and exercise it, to achieve the last two stages of financial freedom. This means not having to wait for the next salary date to plan forward or increase one's spending ability.

FINANCIAL INTELLIGENCE

Financial intelligence is a 3-step process, recognizing potential sources of income, acknowledging and knowing mediums to create money and then implementing your financial intelligence into mediums of cash inflow. Financial intelligence is the key ingredient of financial freedom. There are only two kinds of people in the world, ones who have too little money and ones who have too much money.

FIQ stands for **Financial Intelligence Quotient**. It is the competence to make sensible decisions and measures in managing one's personal finances. The FIQ of an individual is what gives you a boost in your journey towards financial freedom. When there is no financial intelligence or low financial intelligence, an individual cannot create money for himself. A lottery winner often goes broke shortly, because he does not have the financial IQ to grow it or even preserve it.

So how do you become financially intelligent?

First and foremost, the medium is creativity and calculated risks. This allows you to create your own luck. How do you get creative? If you heard the saying "John has 6 hours to chop down the tree, he spends 4 hours sharpening his axe". All individuals, regardless of the age can train their minds, which is undoubtedly your greatest asset. One should train it to be more financially intelligent, so that the rest of your life would be spent with more peace. I know and I hear this a lot "Money does not bring you happiness". On the road to financial freedom, you will find a lot of people who will say something like that. If you chose to ignore them, you have already taken a step further in financial freedom.

Financial intelligence consists of a technical component

- Accounting
- Investing
- Understanding Markets
- Law

Having the ability to read numbers, understanding the science of making money, is not an inherent trait. If you read books like "Rich Dad Poor Dad "or "The Intelligent Investor", you will also agree with the statement that making money is an art. It is important to look at allocation of assets as per the current understanding of the financial markets, technologies, and economies, both from a perspective of sectors or/and recession/boom. Lastly, importance is also given to regulation, which will be later discussed in detail. In short, looking to allocate as per the SEBI/SEC, which are two regulatory bodies for the financial markets.

Why is it important? One might have heard, change is the only constant in life. To be ready for a world where there is change, today your one income source may be lost due to changes (such as the current pandemic – COVID-19), having a strong financial intelligence quotient is not just recognizing and acknowledging the end of a financial source of income, but also recognizing, acknowledging and creating another source of income to counter the loss of a source of income. One cannot hold on to the past, one must adapt in this world. One should look to continuously develop skills and their financial intelligence. Warren Buffett still spends 5 hours a day, sharpening his axe or working on his financial intelligence and knowing more than a Harvard

MBA knows about the world. He is as of today 83 years old; age is no limit to growing your financial intelligence quotient. Schools, colleges, and universities never spend one session on how to be financially intelligent. One must adapt to the self-study path, to grow and prosper in financial intelligence and in finance. Lebron James, possibly the best and the most famous basketball player, has learnt much more from Warren Buffet and other financially intelligent people, compared to what his other fancy MBAs who he hired to correctly advise on financial investments and asset allocation. One more example could be Jeff Bezos, founder, and chairman of Amazon, who is also currently the richest person in the world, gave out the best tip for financial intelligence, per him it is investment in the future. What he conveys through a network of entrepreneurs is venturing in the future, he says that to make real money and know about the true evolution of finance, one must invest in business models which will bring benefit to the future society. Look in your investing environment for your multi-baggers. These multi-baggers are not limited to the stock-market. The rules of the universe say that 90% people make 10% of the money and 10% of the people make 90% of the money. So, 90% people have the philosophy to invest safely, might do it through fixed deposits or a salaried income millennial's favourite i.e. Systematic Investment Plan. The problem with these investments is that they are sanitized, they are created to gain less. These might be good to preserve or look for a little bit of capital appreciation, but these are not wealth creators.

One must really investigate their potential and not limit their capital appreciation. This is where you must have some long conversations with yourself, the kind of conversations you have when you are doing some soul searching. These conversations must be for looking into one's capability to create multiple sources of income. You must go back to the drawing board weigh out your skills and make pros and cons on each potential source of income. This is an exercise needed at whatever age you are. As mentioned earlier, paying yourself first ensures this. If you can pay yourself first and build your assets column, which will generate income or capital appreciation in the future. You would have to pay your liabilities and taxes next, so you would look for ways to pay it off and that will exercise the creativity vertical of the financial intelligence growth. If you pay yourself last, this is pothole on your road to financial freedom, you will settle for lesser savings, lesser capital appreciation and last lesser passive income.

DO NOT FORGET TO PAY YOUR ASSETS (YOURSELF) FIRST. When you pay yourself first, you typically want to invest in paper assets or commonly known as stocks. In today's technology and information age, we have a sea of free-flowing information pertaining to both stock market and the information required to help one understand the movements in the stock market. The stock market does help you in capital appreciation and passive income goals, via stock price growth and dividends. When you are investing in yourself, by building your assets column, on your personal balance sheet, your success or failure is determined by your financial IQ. When you are looking to secure admission in a university, there are commonly standardised tests to test your intelligent quotient, the stock market is no different except that it tests your FQ as opposed to IQ. Today, the stock market is no place for easy and quick money, rewarding strengths like good sales growth, increase in profitability and a decrease in leveraging assets, is a good way forward. In addition, identifying weaknesses like drop in profitability and not enough profitability to cover interest payments, are signs to avoid exposure to the stock positions. When your goal is to be a successful stock market investor, you need to study the health of the organisation, what are the core strengths and weaknesses. One must be able to analyse, how a good year on year growth in profit is more beneficial if it's from the core operations of business, as opposed to if the growth in profit is from non-core operations of business. One must be able to identify the value of a stock's reported earnings in comparison to analyst's expectations. If a stock is growing in value, it might be euphoria, panic or something more permanent. A high FIQ, will make you interpret what the movement of the stock price actually means. This is important to note, when the horizon of the investment is the focus. This study allows your Financial IQ to grow and to be exercised with a higher probability of success.

STUDYING FINANCIAL STATEMENTS

This is probably one of the most important things to learn about investing, before investing. A financial statement of a company reflects its financial health. It is a medium to reflect upon the core strengths and weakness of a firm either financially or even at times non-financially. How to work with financial statements is a skill one has to learn to work with, learning about it is possible for individuals of all ages and for those who don't have sufficient knowledge in the finance vertical. The meaningful interpretation and analysis of balance sheets, income statements, and cash flow statements to discern a company's investment qualities is the basis for smart investment choices. Based on how diversified financial reporting is these days, reporting requirements include preliminary steps that start with becoming aware with certain financial statements features before focusing on individual corporate financials. Highlighting below how instrumental financial statements can be for gaining knowledge about the company.

There are four sections to a company's financial statements: The balance sheet, the income statement, the cash flow statement, and the explanatory notes.

The first step, which is often, called the scoreboard of the company. Sensible investing practices require that we seek out quality companies with strong balance sheets, strong earnings, and positive cash flows. It does not matter if one decides to self-educate to master these skills or depend on an advisor it. The only word of caution I have for the latter audience is that they do ratify that the recommendation from their advisor if not a by-product of a commission sale, set up to benefit the advisor as opposed to the investor. I would like to enunciate here that a basic understanding of the fundamentals is important for both audiences and contrary to popular belief this can be learnt by even those who haven't studied in finance related fields. While at the onset terms such as cash flow, return on investments and profits might bewilder you, over time these same terms promise to serve you well.

As Michael C. Thomsett says in Mastering Fundamental Analysis (1998):

"That there is no secret is the biggest secret of Wall Street and of any specialized industry. Very little in the financial world is so complex that you cannot grasp it. The fundamentals, as their name implies, are basic and relatively uncomplicated. The only factor complicating financial information is jargon, overly complex statistical analysis and complex formulas that don't convey information any better than straight talk."

Even though many textbooks, courses or advisors will say look at the income statement and balance sheet. As a sophisticated investor, who is looking to minimize his risk while gaining the same reward for it, I personally recommend that one pay equal focus to cash flow statements.

It is no secret that 'Cash is King' The cashflow statement literally reflects what is the cash coming in and going out from operations, how it grows or not should be noted. This simple representation also is self-explanatory, as positive cash flow companies are good investments, but growing cash flow positive companies are more attractive. When I research and analyse a company, I often link the sales component of the financial statements to the cash inflow statement, more often they do not match. If that is the case, it could either mean that it has no material impact or it has a material impact. Inflating invoices for higher sales and higher cash conversion cycles are detrimental to the financial health of the company. These actions will lead to higher sales, but no real cash inflow matching the higher sales. Another aspect of cash flow study shows that negative to positive net cash flow also show an opportunity to create multi-baggers.

- Cash flow analysis processes how much money is generated and used by a business during a defined period.

- Cash flow analysis is good because it can be evaluated and contrasted for companies across industries.

- Cash is quantifiable and can be assessed in a medium suitable to everyone.

Undergoing a comparative analysis of two companies, cash flow does stand as a universal comparative trait. It is difficult to fake. There are many dodgy practices used to overstate profits, to falsely increase the value of a business, to make it appear more attractive to the naked eye. It is commonly recognized as a store of value. You do not have to convince anyone as to the value. A venture might have a very high paper value, but maybe cash flow week. Everyone accepts cash as a strength.

The presentation of a company's situation financially, as displayed in its financial statements, is biased by management's estimates and judgments. In compliant conditions, the management is meticulously honest and frank, while the internal and external auditors have become stricter, post the banking collapse in 2008-2009 crisis. Whether they were honest or not, the sketchiness and numerous loopholes that can are innately found in the accounting process, convey that one should take a questioning and sceptical approach when you begin your study of financial statements. This is a statutory warning which should not be ignored and a key ingredient of financial intelligence.

Our discussion category is about what the numbers of a corporation's financial statements are telling us. The numbers in a company's financial statements mirror the company's business, products, services, and important macro level fundamental changes. These numbers and the financial ratios or indicators derived from them are simpler to understand if you can interpret the realities of the business model. Aside from the core financials, there is also a management commentary section, which tells us about what the management's vision was for the year post its Annual General Meeting. When you view it in hindsight, you will be able to decipher how much has or has not been achieved against previously set targets. The management commentary is a part of the annual prospectus, is like any other prospectus you receive once you purchase something. This prospectus tells us about the condition of the economy, the industry, competitive considerations, market forces, technological change, the management quality, and the workforce cannot directly be presented in a company's financial statements. Investors need to be able to tell if the information mentioned will provide a positive or negative future outcome. This will allow you to understand, whether it is a good investment or not.

EXERCISE- Look up the company that you are keen to better understand , start with an arbitrary search of "XYZ's Financial statement", look at the information outcome and note down information, have a process which could help you understand the company more closely. Look up a financial glossary for any terms which would help you interpret the outcome with the most clarity, link the management's commentary to the numbers. See the ratios, which could be as simple as net profit margin to the cash conversion cycle. The kind of ratio's you should investigate are debt/equity to know about the leverage of the company. The other important ratio is Net/Gross Profit Margin, which indicates the profitability. When you are comparing, also look at interest coverage and assets to liabilities ratio. Look up the terms you don't understand, look up the formulae you weren't able to interpret, the more things you don't know, the more time it's going to take, but the outcome is going to be more fruitful to move up the ladder in the road to financial freedom.

THE INVESTMENT PHILOSOPHY

I believe in enforcing capital preservation and then aiming for capital appreciation over time. I like to invest with a clear investment philosophy and a set of principle, which act as my disciplined guided forces of investment. They have changed with time and experience, but the core principles and philosophies have stayed the same.

I look at companies with greater certainty of earnings. Heavy reliance is on the focus on towards superior and consistent quality of earnings vs the mere quantum of earnings growth. My philosophy is fuelled with the notion that quality is not cheap, if you can identify quality now after this exercise, there have been many people who have identified this strength in quality before. If you are learning about this stock and also about identifying stocks, there are already experts with better skills and have identified the output of your same analysis When a lot of people buy a particular stock, just like the demand-supply metric, the price of the stock rises. So, the ideology behind my next investment criteria is high quality stocks at reasonable price over inferior quality stocks at arithmetically cheaper prices. So how do I go about that, I tend to identify the pricing in the value, not valuing the current price for purchase. I look at models and create outcomes of where the business will go on forth to know the intrinsic value of the stock. There is an identification of companies, which are either value or growth, the former are companies with proven track records and the latter is companies who have yet to prove their track record. I have a unique philosophy of identifying growth companies at value prices, which means high potential companies at not very high prices. I am a strong believer in disciplined investing, I adopt the systematic investment plan, every month on certain dates an amount gets directly debited from my bank account and goes straight into stocks or mutual funds. Systematic investment plans are adopted using mutual funds as the investment vehicle, and my choice of mutual funds tend to be skewed towards mid-small market capitalisation companies, but this can vary as per your risk and return quotient, so read up on an Investment philosophy statement, download a free one and determine your risk quotient today. Always invest with the interest of compounding returns, just as we learned in our mathematical class in school, the golden rule is that power of compounding outweighs the outcomes of simple interest investing.

I also look at the material size of the opportunity in growth of my investment and research on the management quality to manage it to deliver the superior returns I want, I can 80-90% times trust, Mukesh Ambani, Chairman of Reliance Industries, to deliver good returns for the stock, because of his superior management quality, but I need to still research on the other management if I have a longer horizon. One of the key learnings I have from this stock is that superior quality of business, is indicated by the strong earnings growth. So, take your favourite stock/stocks, and start noting yes/no to the criteria.

To further narrow stock-selection for your investment, one should look at the size of the opportunity, which is the foundation for continual growth of profits, creating a compounding foundation on which a large value creation lies. The investment should not be on how big the business is today, the focus should be what it can be in the future. An opportunity basket of stocks is when the sector should be strong and the company's capability to maximize and exploit the opportunity should be evident in it is past. When you're evaluating a company's quality of business, focus on persistent and superior capital efficiency, that is a metric which reflects upon the future outcome of investment. One important quality criterion is the earnings growth of a firm, I personally believe that this trait is not self-sufficient to identify a multi-bagger of the future. Wealth preservation is more evolving as a compulsion for investors, my personally belief is that quality of business and quality of management are the two major parameters for capital protection and capital appreciation. When we consider quality of management, we investigate how capital has been distributed on an efficiency parameter. The bigger the conglomerate is, with diverse industries, the riskier it is, as a company in an Auto sector has also a Telecom sector exposure, this introduces a conglomerate discount. It is impossible that a company with diverse exposures, will always do well, but it can be that the same company can have negative returns in all sectors during a bad time. I am not saying do not invest in these companies, I want you to be able to detect the companies which do that and limit exposure on the same. Conglomerates are often chosen as investment vehicles for investors, who are looking for capital protection, with a slight upside potential. The upside or the growth potential of an investment portfolio is derived from a rewarding capital allocation. The management of a business is the most important factor of both the growth story and the survival of the company. Quality growth of a business must be secular, predictable, less volatile and businesses having character simple enough to understand, especially from the perspective of a first-time investor. A company's cash-flow strength has and will be important aspect for the company's growth story, as indicated before in the earlier chapters, it is the most overlooked aspect of the financial statement analysis. I personal believe the famous P/E ratio, is not the correct metric to decode an investment's intrinsic value, maybe considered with many other ratios, but solely not strong enough.

So how do I narrow down on a few stocks from my checklist?

As explained before, a strong management is a unique selling point as an investment criterion. I analyse Indian Entrepreneurial businesses of good size, superior quality, and high growth at fair valuation. I follow a very rigorous, disciplined, strong filters-based investment approach, while embracing value-creating traits. When you are looking for the strong management, research on the vision, high standards of governance, wisdom and demonstrated capital allocation and capital distribution skills. The superior quality of management unlocks the preservation of value and high growth is sought to achieve expansion of value. The promoters or the senior management, who have adequate skin in the game ensure that there is alignment of other management and shareholder interests. I believe family businesses on the listed space is large component of the promoter driven and successfully driven ventures. There is a lot of passion, commitment and conviction towards the investment objectives and the mission of the companies. The investment horizon is a longer term, than other business, they have a lot of skin in the game, to align with the interests of shareholders. With their dynamic leadership, they can spot opportunities early. They do tend to score well on innovation and intellectual capital. I am going to further break this down using filters to identify these investment vehicles.

These are the filters for the diagram, I am going to use are size of opportunity, financial performance, management quality, income growth, quality of business value added.

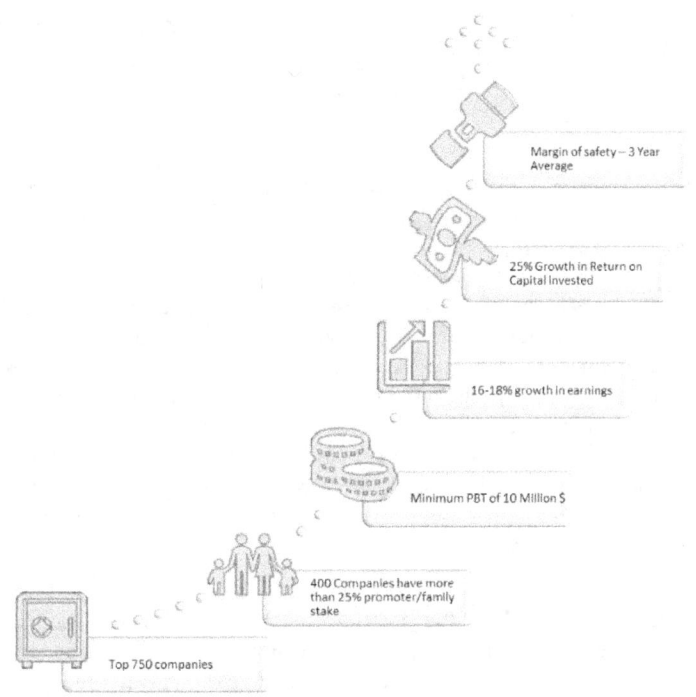

It's size of the opportunity, management quality, financial performance, income growth and quality of business value added for me or any other Indian investor would be majorly the top 500 companies in terms of market capitalisation. For analysing the financial performance, I would have a minimum Profit before tax criteria of 10 Million $. For evaluation of the management quality, looking specifically at the integrity, vision, execution, and capital allocation skills, to fulfil the management quality trait. For income growth, I would like to evaluate firstly without additional capital allocated, what is the yield of the investment and whether it would grow at a minimum 16-18 % or not. 16-18% annually, is a minimum return scale for my investments.

The next filter, looks at the excellence of commerce, which highlights return on the capital invested by the shareholders over 3 – 5 year period, this should aggregate at least 25% as, the return to investors is typically after tax, with a 25% tax bracket, we could then yield returns of my 16-18% scale. The last filter is value, this is something which requires the most analysis, we need to take an average of the 3 year's price of the stock and derive the value of the stock at its mode and higher quartile to know the potential of a stock, this is the last filter so the output can vary. These all filters are followed EXACTLY in the order presented so that the portfolio can yield the maximum returns, this narrows the criteria significantly. Try this exercise and do it repetitively, to get the correct understanding of a stock portfolio. The study of companies should be done for at least 10 years, on parameters like sales, profit, return of capital employed and value added to the investment (from sales not capital infusion). My personal belief and analysis for a period of 30 days on the mentioned criteria's, proved to me (it can vary for you) that the stocks after those five filters, had continued dominance even today post 10 years of analysis. They are faster growing compared to other business, where promoters do not have as much skin in the game. They have above average operating performance and stronger capital efficiency. The last but not the least, is the criteria that these filters have fulfilled, is the fact that these businesses or stocks are the biggest wealth creators.

Entrepreneurial firms are present across vibrant and emerging sectors, they identify sunrise sectors and include a blend of manufacturing as well as services. They also are shown to have a tight cost control, the highest return on equity and a higher business operating efficiency. The decisions tend to be speedy and dynamic, as they are operating in a competitive environment. Every investment you make, must be weighed by both the risks, and returns. We have only mentioned about the returns yet, the risks cannot be ignored. The risks associated with investments are that the decision making is usually centralized, so a top-down approach is followed, which can limit flexibility. Nepotism is a negative factor for succession planning, as the son/daughter is usually in line for managing the business for the next generations. These risks associated have been eliminated or reduced, by the last 3 filters, as capital allocation, and value creation, helps identify business with the strongest management quality, not every listed family business is good for investment. Getting the right filter at the right time of the analysis is important to identify value.

After half a decade in the portfolio management services industry, there are ways I have formed disciplined buying and selling mechanisms to pre-decide any stop loss and also not allowing any single stock to become too big in percentage of my portfolio.

I buy businesses, which have a relatively good safety of margin, which means undervalued stocks, they are just sentimentally weak, but vice-versa fundamentally. Believing in compliance and integrity, will hold further importance to your portfolio's growth story. I believe in the people who are managing my investments, the promoters and the senior management are also following the same grounds, for beginners in investment, google about the company and check the auditors remarks on the financial statements, to review any noise on compliance. The next rule of investment is knowing how to limit your losses, by enforcing stop-loss targets. If you have sell targets the minute your investment in the stock falls below 15% and also have a sell cap on any stock, when any stock crosses 10% of your entire stocks portfolio, you will have successfully reduced the risk of your positions.

Reflect on the exercise, done in the previous topic if your company fits these, if it does you know several parameters of fundamental investing have been fulfilled. If you are looking to invest, you will need cash, don't limit it to 20% of your salary. Your personal investment philosophy ideally and eventually should be to use your passive income or side hustles to pay your bills and use your active income to create more assets, by investing in yourself in multiple ways and not being restricted to only financial assets. There are multiple ways, where you can break the monotonous cash flow pattern, which dictates your investments. When you earn more, you can invest more, which will allow you take a giant leap in your journey towards financial freedom. Earning more (side hustles), does involve more time commitment than your 9-5, it surely helps you in your liquidity, which will help you in your first 3 stages of financial freedom. My personal recommendation, is to have a goal of doubling your income to invest more in yourself and in your financial assets.

CREATING MORE INCOME

THE HUSTLER- BREAK THE RAT RACE AND WIN IN LIFE

"Living off one source of income, is one step away from poverty"

Having multiple sources of income, will allow you flexibility to achieve your goals-based investing plans. On the downside, if you leave/quit/are fired from your job, you have a cushion of funds to depend upon. There are many consensuses on the apt number for sources of income, I personally believe 5 would suffice, contrary to the "7" number. The main reason for this contradiction, is building passive incomes requires a significant time commitment, not just on building them but also on building skills necessary to acquire them. We have already spoken about how, portfolio income (stock price appreciation) will be considered as a secondary source of income. Furthermore, the main reason why you are building sources of income is for freedom to do what you want, devoting all the time to your work and lesser time to simple and best joys of life, for me: family, my partner and my friends, is contradicting the whole motive of financial freedom. If your starting today, Mr. X's advice would be to start with building 2 external sources of income. You should be aiming to build 5 sources of income over the next 3 years, as there would be a time commitment attached with building the base to allow side hustle incomes to flow into your checking account.

The next step is how to start, firstly one must be clear between passive and active income. An active income is like your core business or your job, where you are paid for the time you put in. A passive income is money that keeps hitting your cash inflows projects, even If you are not dedicating hours to the same. You might not need 5 sources of income; you can have 5 ways of making money from the same source of income. You could be a blogger, can get paid to promote, teach, or even advise on your specialities. Further illustration was provided by how Akshay Kumar magnified his income by creating 5 mediums of income from the same source i.e. Film Making.

In today's world anything you can do or like doing or even are doing, can lead to a cash cow for your effort or interest. Allow me to give you Mr. X's sources of income, to allow you some perspective on the discussed material:

- Working in a firm Active Income, gets Paid 1800$ a month
- An active investor in stocks, and buys all throughout the year – 850$ a month of financial assets building
- Helping start-ups fundraise, Freelancing CFO – Active Income, gets paid 300$ a month
- Owning a franchise - Passive Income – makes 250$ a month
- E-commerce - Passive Income – makes 600$ a month

Mr. X dedicated his most hours in a day to source number 1. He is passionate about investing in stocks and his career revolves around that. Putting into perspective source number 3, 4 and 5 is what we define as his side hustles. He builds them over the weekends or after working hours. One more thing, I would like to highlight from observing Mr. X, is that he was working on his skill set to improve sources 1,2 and 3, by pursuing CFA, learning Spanish and taking up sales course, he's at the last level of the charter. When you grow your skillset, you understand that it is an important medium of developing sources of income. If Mr X did not sharpen his Spanish skills or gave up after failing the Charter exam or did not pursue the sales course because it was worth 500$ he would not have grown in his journey towards financial freedom. He was working hard enough on increasing clients for each vertical of income, by dedicating 2 hours a day to each one of them, that allowed him to reach financial freedom faster. One must also diversify their income sources, like Mr. X had developed a stream of income from a different industry, like source number 5, which was e-commerce based and his other sources of income are basically from the finance industry. There was zero correlation between the finance and e-commerce-based income, which meant he would be protected anytime if the industry is hit badly.

A side hustle is not an easy task as it requires one to break the monotonous life most of us reading today are living. It involves creating a passive income, going beyond your daily 40 hours work week. A side hustle is defined as a mostly passive income base, it revolves around putting hours to reward you financially, even when you are not actively putting in hours to earn the same. Though not completely defined by this, some can also be active incomes. Every side hustle starts with an idea! People believe there is a lack of good ideas and that allows them to be lazy and avoid hustles. The best aspect of these side hustle ideas is that many do not require a huge initial investment or even necessarily a highly specialized skill set. These ideas are not all million-dollar income streams, but each one can add to your current cash inflows These are worth anywhere from 25$ to 25000$ a month, all based on hours and effort into them.

Let us look at the most common PASSIVE INCOME ideas

- Youtuber- Create videos online which can be a display of skills, even as simple as fitness videos
- Blogging- Via videos, websites, pictures or any other medium, can help you present marketing to a niche audience
- Teaching- I am always helping finance enthusiasts, what I have learnt over my career, create a video online displaying your skill and sell to an audience for the correct price
- Online surveys - Filling in surveys can help add to the kitty as well.
- Flipping items on amazon, e-bay, flipkart- Trading margins can be a cool 50-250 per trade
- Driving- Have a spare few hours over the weekend or after work, best decision to use that idle cars, drivers earn a minimum 50$ a day (that's part time)
- Invest in REIT's, allows you to increase your passive income exposure by as little as 1000$ (for a cool 10$ a month cash flow plus a chance of appreciation)
- Airbnb Housing- Have an extra room at home or an office space to lease, best medium to create cash flow for fixed payment for already possessed assets.
- Renting your car- Using public transport to work and back, why not rent out your car for the weekdays, Get Around delivers 25$ a day for car usage.
- Cooking/Baking- Something which I have personally taken up as a hobby (Thanks to COVID-19), can be used as a blogging, teaching or delivery medium.
- Being a Task Master- Following up with clients to ensure they complete their tasks to reach their goals e.g. TaskRabbit.
- Tutoring- It can be in person or on digital platforms which can pay more (based on customers) like Udemy.
- Kindle Publishing – E-books cover topics for all geographies, cultures, personality development, art etc. Can make 10$ to 1000$ a month, based on quantity and quality.
- Fiverr- Every Freelancer's dream for getting their skill sets to a larger audience. No limit on the money you can make here.
- Dividend Investing- Warren Buffet makes close to 700 million $ a year from dividends.

Well there are probably 100's of more ideas, but since everyone's skillset isn't the same, you could look at what your skill set can deliver for you. One should really go back to the drawing board and create verticals via which they can create cash flows. Side hustles require extra hours, as cliché it might sound 9-5 pays your bills, but your 6-10 builds your empire. One must learn to not depend on one source of income. There are many risks of that. It could occur from job loss, disability, sudden expense, pursuing an opportunity.

Earn that extra buck

Earning more money, is way beyond a luxury or optional, it is a way of living, especially COVID-19 proves why it is essential to not be dependent on one source of income. 20 % companies, have either reduced salaries, shut down or filed for bankruptcy. If the COVID-19 economic scenario and already present mounting job losses have taught us anything, it is that job security is not mandatory for everyone. Unfortunately for 90%people, their only dependence on money, is their 9-5, which can be a dangerous way to live. This COVID-19 has highlighted the importance of an emergency cash fund and a need for another source of income. If married, couples are fortunate enough to have each other's income source to depend on for their livelihood. I would further highlight below why it is a necessity to have multiple sources of income.

- Emergency funds- COVID-19 is a special case, where earnings can drop and costs still have to maintained (salaries, rent etc), having a safety net of funds will allow one to be prepared for the worst scenario. I would suggest at least 6 months of expenditures set aside. Another case would be the emergency health cost scenario which could put you in jeopardy if you don't have this fund set aside, it could be as urgent as immediate, this is a must and the first reason why one should have multiple sources of income. When you do not have to touch your savings and not be totally dependent for that salary to be credited, is a bonus and also highlights why it is not a luxury, but an absolute necessity to have multiple sources of income.

- Debt killer- Many people take up on debt to fuel purchases or investments, have one or more (the merrier) sources of income will allow one to be flexible enough to pay off debts and allow one to not be growing his or her debt, as interest can be a real expensive mistress. When you have lesser debt, it will accelerate your path towards financial freedom.

- Investment for the new vertical of income- To create another source of income, one must make investment to create a cash cow. Be it the money or the time, both investments must be necessary. Another stream of income will create a faster roadmap to financial freedom and an escape route from the 9-5 rat race.

- Savings should be larger than spending – Why reduce your savings and be stingy, when you can create another source and do whatever you want financially and without depending on one salary.

- Overseeing your income- Not getting a raise or that ideal income from your job? Try hustling to out earn your competition, because firms might be going through a bad phase or you might be a victim of office politics, where growth is not as soon as your next expense.

- Wanderlust vibes – Have a wish list which encompasses of travelling and seeing all those places, maybe even with a spouse/family, having a 9-5 to pay your regular bills and having another cash flow to build a fund to travel, will allow you to attend a tomorrow land festival without waiting for a tomorrow's salary.

- Unemployment- Jobs are not safe, nothing is secure today. One can lose a job overnight, even someone like Amazon (promoted by the world's richest person) could sack people overnight, having a safety net is a survival kit for a job loss.

- Purchases- Fancy a new car or a new luxury item, you do not have to look at the calendar to see when your next salary day is to allow yourself to buy the luxury. You would avoid debt (credit card or a loan) for the same, which reduces interest owned.

- Rule number 1 of portfolio management (diversify)- having multiple cash flows allows you to diversify cash flow needs. If one cash flow is delayed or missed, another one or maybe more are there to help you pay bills. If all cash flows come in at the right time your bank account grows as hoped for.

There is no set limit as to the number of income streams you could have. One should look at the return on investment (time and money) to denote whether to pursue it and to what extent. There are many important benefits of creating many income streams to decrease your risk of having your main source of income suddenly disappear. Even if your alternative sources of income cannot cover your monthly expenses, they can at least help reduce the impact of a job loss or other unexpected expense. If you are lucky enough, these income streams could potentially do more than just supplementing your income. They could grow your assets base, which should be every millennial's dream.

Look back at the diagram, we have already covered how to reach stage 3 in your journey towards financial freedom, to move on to stage 4 and onwards, there are few aspects which we need to cover. Moving up the pyramid of financial freedom, you often question the fact that is seems impossible, when in reality, it's the total opposite. It has become easier over time.

WHY IS FINANCIAL FREEDOM EASIER NOW, THAN EVER?

Today whatever venture, hustle, or skill you're looking to get remunerated for has become easier to exploit for higher income. One might even question old age thoughts like work ethic and long working hours. The internet today is a centre of all information, Mr. X has acquired over 90% of his clients and 60% of his sales from leads generated online. The internet is creating more business for everyone. Earlier when wealth could be inherited or acquired it used to be next to impossible to create wealth from scratch. We are in an information age, where data is king. This allows any individual to create a market from the internet which creates wealth. For example, Jeff Bezos, Founder and Chairman of AMAZON. He created wealth from selling books in his garage to selling anything and literally everything online. The internet created the world's richest man and the largest company in the world, who is all set to even be the first trillion-dollar man next decade. The technology changes allow innovation to fast track almost anything, this fast-paced change stimulates the economy. Today the major change in technology, is the driving force of many economies. It does not take too long to notice that the major contribution to the growth of many billionaires and many newly wealthy citizens has happened via technology. Way back in the early 90's, wealth was created by the rich and powerful, who also managed the media mainly. But in today's age with Facebook, Instagram, LinkedIn, YouTube, Twitter and many other mediums like that, the power of media is in our hands. One needs a smartphone/ personal computer and good internet connection to make a buck. As people become richer and wealthier, they obviously gain access to more excess cash, which can be used to invest in other start-ups or even listed companies, which further creates more money. This money creation and the fast movement of money is what has contributed to 2 trillion $ of new money last year. The new revolution to the world economy and the emergence of multiple mediums to create wealth which is technology, has created fortunes with minimum time and effort. The internet makes it easier for every one of us reading this book to become wealthier. To take the first step, it doesn't matter whether you are working for yourself or you are an employee at a firm, no matter the size of the firm your employed with, there are strategies which will help you increase your capabilities of earning more than you are earning right now. These skills are learned from the world wide web medium, so there would be emergence of tech skills in your bouquet of skills. If you know a few traits in the digital medium, is a sure shot way to put yourself higher in another income bracket. The good news about these skills, is that they can be leveraged at office, for work or outside work in your side hustles.

If you are not from a business or finance background, but more from the technical background, it should not affect your aim of financial freedom. Designing and developing websites is in huge need right now, and this likely to grow to new heights with the number of mobile users increasing every single day. The process of designing and developing games is not easy, especially the ones with a great user experience, which is why good mobile designers and developers are in such high demand. The great reality check is that you do not have to go back to computer engineering classes to learn these skills. If you already have some general web design skills, mobile design is not a huge hurdle. One can have a side hustle in practically any tech-related vertical of operation, from coding to designing to social media management. The intriguing part of this side hustle is that it can let you build up a customer base, without having you quitting your 9 am to 5 pm job. One can use this side hustle, to increase the amount of active income a month. One of the most growing verticals of tech, which is rewarding, glamorous and interesting is content marketing. It as simple and as fun a side hustle can be, it includes maintaining a company's blog or social media accounts. Probably the most common freelancers are the website designers, they design websites for clients in specific industries. Tying this into your day job can be a great way to reduce the gap and give yourself a good advantage over the other members of your team i.e. the 33% of the people. For illustrative purposes, if you work in hospitality by day, you might specialize in designing websites for hotels, bars, restaurants, and other hospitality verticals because you understand how the hospitality industry works. One major thing to be cautious of is that your side hustle is not taking business away from your day job employer. Protecting this interest, cannot cause a conflict of interest. There are all different kind of hustles, you can do to find the correct fit between freelancing while you're employed at a firm, and still earn income and a medium of wealth creation in the information age, where more money is created.

By now, you would have a fairly strong idea how financial freedom and financial intelligence are correlated. With the information age, growing even further, one can achieve financial freedom more easily. There are still some skills, which you have to develop to be able to achieve financial freedom, with the roadmap you have created. You need to be able to leverage these skills correctly, to become financially independent. There are some unique skills a majority of financially independent individuals possess. These skills develop and further strengthen your financial IQ, which will result in more wealth. But you have to take the step of developing these skills or further enhancing them, this can be your biggest step towards financial independence.

HOW DO I START TODAY?

BY SKILL DEVELOPMENT- SHARPEN THE AXE BEFORE YOU CHOP DOWN THE TREE

Sales learning

I have had friends all my life who have discredited my sales role in the financial markets, the idea of sales not just in banking but also in other financial industries has been tarnished over the years. I was selling advice on the financial markets, what I was doing is advising clients on investments, I was reaching out to clients/prospects to display skills. Sales is the most important part of a company, be it financially or non-financially, in fact if you have done the exercise in the earlier chapters regarding the financial statements, it is the first step. At a certain point in your profession, even if you are not into sales, you're going to have to sell a little, whether it's your hard work on your side hustle, your business group, or yourself. One cannot really learn about sales, without selling something i.e. the selling experience. Today's parents and students look at sales as a below par job, but it is really the driving force for all major companies and I believe you have to sell what your good at, so that your prospects and clients know your good at it. I recommend reading an international best seller for some serious motivation on sales, "How I raised myself from failure to success in selling" by Frank Bettger. Selling is basically moving somebody or something towards action. If you look at your daily schedule, from internal meetings with peers to conference calls with clients, almost all your verbal or written communications involve some type of selling. One should be able to reflect upon conversations when a sale did not happen, or a business idea failed and note down the shortcomings. One should also be able to be in the other person's shoes, to know how to respond rather than react, responding is always positive and reacting is always negative. I recommend for both sales and non-sales professionals that they should do their research to figure out what is critical to your counter party and what problems they're trying to solve, both personally and from a business point of view. If you are able to seek permission before you speak about your product or a service, this automatically moves you from a sleazy salesman, who is meeting the client for commission, to an advisor or a friend who is helping the counter party solve a problem. In "Rich dad and Poor Dad", the author Robert Kiyosaki mentioned, his book was a sensation, with over 200 million copies sold, because he was a best-selling author and not necessarily the best writing author. If you are looking to start easy, learning what not to do is always easier and faster, than learning what to do be the best salesperson. Do not speak too much, do not go to measures which illustrate something exaggerated. Keep the discussion pointed and focused upon how YOU can help YOUR counter party and not the other way around. My next focus would be e-courses to grow your sales skillset, courses about selling with advice and professional development opportunities will help in growing your income. Even if you are already selling, learning how to better at it, is always a lifelong competitive advantage in the field of sales. Apart from online sales programs, you can take free certification courses through vendors like Coursera or my recommendation if you have the long-term vision or if your already in sales is to take up the Grant Cardone sales training program, you can view the website to see what budget and time commitment would best suit you.

Self-discipline

Practicing self-discipline is important, not just to be financially free, but also to become your best version. Establishing a budget is a fairly easy but committing to it is where individuals can and have failed in the past. Post long working hours, one does tend to give in to the short-term gratification of ordering from outside, rather than having the nutritious food at home. When one is out in restaurants, bars or even group vacations with friends you will indulge more than you ever do, because you as an individual have less self-discipline and can be motivated to splurge more than planned, because you got carried away. You must focus on learning how to improve your self-discipline, eliminating or reducing temptations, do not shop every weekend, so that you do not repeat what you wore. The fear of a few comments from others, should not affect your saving and investing plans. We are all human, so one should keep budgeting for tiny treats, this can also help keep you encouraged to stay put to your financial goals without feeling disadvantaged.

Organized

It can be challenging to become financially free if you skip payments. When you choose to or force to pay your dues later than the due date, it can result in fines or, in the case of credit cards, higher interest rates. Not maintaining records, can create problems and will lead to an empty savings or current account because of the underrated impact of overdraft fees. If you are an individual living on a tight budget, those extra costs can make it challenging to increase savings and increase assets and reduce your time to financial freedom.

Be it today or a decade ago not many people are organized, because they are messy and often lazy, there are many ways online where you can create an auto debit, receive notifications when your balance in the account is low, or when there are payments due or when you can divest to build more assets. Get used to starting a financial journal or diary and keep your statements of investment printed. Start a filing system, keep important documents within reach. If the mode of data is electronic, make sure you have them saved with an extra copy, be it over a pen drive, or a cloud or even in your personal email.

Logical thinking

There are many fakes and swindlers in all most every industry, they use the not so easy to understand investment products to your disadvantage. It is not necessary, it's always a scam, we still do get texts (at least in India) that require you to do a certain thing or pay a certain amount to get a lottery or something like that, there are still 5000+ cases of the same. When it comes to investments, it can also be a dishonest broker posing as an advisory. These brokers can try to push investment products which can be to your disadvantage and can be financially painful.

Logical thinking is important skill to develop to prevent yourself from losing money to dreadful investment products. Whenever you are making an investment plan and pursuing it, make it a point to understand the functions and features of the investment product. Often look at the person offering the opportunity, to see if his benefit proceeds are larger than yours. Online shopping is an all-time favourite for all millennials, more people will be shopping online in the future as well, and more scam artists will be there to steal your information and money. If you see an email or a call regarding something which sounds like a scam, DO NOT take the bait. We live in the world of Facebook and Instagram, make sure the people you relate to are genuine and have physical existence, not just limited to digital existence. One must regularly update their passwords to protect information. Please protect yourself from advertisements, which teach you to make money online, no it is not going to be this easy, the journey embarked towards financial freedom. Always use private wi-fi or broadband for online purchase, using public wi-fi leaks information to online hackers. Do not fall prey to these make quick money Instagram self-proclaimed Gurus.

Second language

Probably the second most important skill to develop, after sales learning. But when combined with sales learning, this can grow your income multi-fold.

Today the major contribution to creativity, after technology is the proficiency of a second language. Even business school graduates often allude to foreign language courses as some of the most appreciated courses in college because of skills developed to addressing problems with a solution. If you are from an English-Speaking nation, exposure to Spanish, Chinese and even German language can enlarge one's vision of the world communication, increases one's capabilities and make them more flexible and adaptable to business environments to understand customers and target bases. Today as immigration is on the rise, we need to prepare for change in almost all business communities. Any individual, business or economy is more effective and responsible in a multi-cultural environment, if they can speak multiple languages, there is no downside in learning another language. The more languages you know, if not access, the exposure is huge. It is possible to understand new financial markets and probably a new target audience for your expertise, bilingual skills are appreciated for growth.

One important and quickest impact in measurable terms, would be the impact on your personal network. This magnifies and upgrades your network. As earlier mentioned in this book, the more people are there in your network, the more money you can make. No debate is even necessary, whatsoever to the advantages of learning a foreign language in terms of amplifying the gateway to increase your network either professionally or personally. You can expect people to generally have confidence in you more if you can speak their language. When you are speaking a language, a potential customer can understand, he can have access to you. When you speak the same language as your customer, they treat you as their own. Two examples will amplify the importance of being bilingual, regionally Gujarati is considered a good language to know for Indians, who are trading in the stock markets or even consumer goods. Internationally, Spanish and Chinese are said to create new markets for interaction, business school candidates can interact with batchmates to understand culture, economies, and business environment better. So, knowing how to speak their language, makes you appear 'like one of their own'. This should allow you to gain your potential network's trust more than an individual who is typical stranger who does not communicate in the same language. When you speak the same language, a similar cultural connection is created. Learning a language like Chinese, has proven to open you up to many professionals and individuals who can work together, this significantly broadens one's group of beneficial contacts. These are individuals you could both do business with or become a mediator or a broker (for commission), creating an additional source of revenue from the service offering.

In today's global world, learning a foreign language is essential to your success in another country. Learning the German language, helps in employability, as per recent studies. - FORBES

Studying a different language is not very easy, it requires patience, perseverance, and practice. However, people who speak two or more than two languages, have been shown to have a superior capability to have access to a more logical and coherent analogy of communications, than individuals who can only speak one language. When you know a different language, you can avoid trouble and enhance probability of good verticals (closing a deal faster), it allows you to utilize your entire logical capacity. So, what this to you monetarily and non-monetarily is improves your judgment and fastens the process of coming to a decision.

When you do not have to go to google translate every time you are travelling or conversing with anyone who could be a potential client. Possessing the knowledge of how to switch between two languages without stopping your response ability, does bring a sure shot profit. Moreover, an enhanced awareness, like knowing "My name is Dev" is "Me llamo Dev", can improve memory abilities. Knowing a foreign language, like Spanish or Chinese, one can become proficient at noticing and concentrating on non-highlighted but important aspects of business importance. One distinct advantage from knowing a foreign language makes you a skilled at identifying ambiguous information, this is particularly critical in deals and interaction with prospects and alliances.

These abilities can make you a superior speaker and a superior listener. This makes you a better listener and communicator, than your peers or colleagues. If there is a job or task at hand, which requires a better communicator, you know a bi-linguistic candidate (which should be you) is going to selected. With online mediums like Coursera and Udemy, learning a foreign language is good and you can notice your mind grow in as little time as a fortnight. One more bonus advantage of learning a second (foreign) language, is the enhancement of your multitasking abilities. One can shift easily between two or more totally different activities. When you discover a new language and culture, it is natural to compare, to help develop a pattern.

At the rate at which firms are becoming a part of the globalisation parameter, sticking to just knowledge of just one language, can be your biggest mistake to in your professional life. Today we consume more foreign products, than domestic. Just as it would be a disadvantage to stick to one country for your customer base, it would be a disadvantage to stick to one language. You would be doing yourself a whole lot of disservice. Obviously, gaining a second language skill is difficult, and an exasperating activity. That is the only disadvantage, but with unlimited upside. Proficiencies like problem solving, interaction with abstract concept will rise because you know more than language. Foreign Language study creates more positive attitudes and less prejudice toward people who are different. Analytical skills improve when students study a foreign language. Business skills plus foreign language skills make an employee more valuable and employable in the marketplace. When you are dealing with another culture, the audience can gain a more profound understanding of their own culture.

I believe all these skills combined will help you grow individually and financially. The day you stop learning, is the day you stop growing. Learning skills alone, can be boring or exhaustive at times, this can be done with your friend, colleague and even better if it's with your partner. The important thing to note about skill learning is also with whom you get to exhibit or learn these skills for. At the end of the day, is how much network can you grow with these skills.

NETWORKING – THE UNDERRATED WEALTH CREATOR

I look at the greatest friendships both in terms of age and wealth, Bill Gates, and Warren Buffet. These 2 charismatic and wealthy individuals have more than 150 billion $ in combined wealth. They are both investors, Bill Gates own a significant number of Berkshire Hathaway shares, while Warrant Buffet, has invested significantly in the Bill and Melinda Foundation. Over seminars and many interviews of their in-depth conversations, made me rethink the relationships I had with many people. These podcasts and videos gave me a reality check, of which friendships are financially toxic. They helped me identify what was the problem in either me or them, helped me identify a pattern of decisions which led to my early 20s being not as financially secure as my current age is.

The key takeaways were-

- By choosing the right group of friends, you can push yourself to achieve bigger professional goals, Buffett and Gates say "You will move in the direction of the people that you associate with," says Buffett, who recently addressed a group of students along with Gates.

When you are in the early-to-mid phases in your career, your growth also depends on your network. My mentor now heading one of the BIG 4, told me his first job was selling credit cards. He mentioned how he would have all his friends get involved and support him. I reflected in my personal life if people would purchase what I was selling. I was shocked to have a moment of realization of the lack of support on the same. Let me highlight, it wasn't the question about affording, as I was privileged enough to go to school, college and live in a decent society and had friends I grew up with, could afford what I was advising on, without a pinch in their wallet. It was pretty clear, that affordability was not the problem, but the realization was not because of the product I was selling, but the fact that it was me selling, the fact that there was no intent to buy from me. But I am also glad to recognize those friends who did and recommended, those people have stuck by me even now. They have benefitted greatly, as I improved my skills, education and got more experienced, their portfolio of investments grew and beat the benchmark (in India, its Sensex), 80% of the time.

- Supporters - "Some friends do bring out the best in you," the Microsoft co-founder says, "and so it's good to invest in those friendships."

As mentioned earlier, we are living in an information age, there is an abundance of data, the most major contributor for this is social media. In today's age, 90% of you reading this book right now have access to or at least have used social media at least once in their life. Today support can be done via two-three simple clicks, as you hear many YouTubers say "Like Share and Subscribe", even though you have 100s or 10s of friends, not all the 'friends' who you hangout or spend time with, would share and promote your work for you. It is just a few clicks, or maybe lesser i.e. share button. You must build connections who truly support you. I have friends from my university on a WhatsApp group, this was back in 2013 – 2014 I had started a venture. Back then Facebook, Instagram, LinkedIn and snapchat, were social media mediums which were very famous back then, with a social engagement of close to a billion people. I had shared just one message in the group promoting my venture, to help me promote it, it did not cost a single penny, nor did it take a minute, but out of the 15 members, only 7 people shared the message and out of which 2, happen to be very good friends to date, took the effort of recommending and writing their review on the product and the promoter(yours truly).

The 33% rule

100% of your time divided by 3, you get 33, that is the amount of time you need to spend with 3 types of people.

Firstly, are those people who are above you in maturity, hierarchy, earnings, or age. Secondly are the people who fall at par with you in the same verticals. The third and last range of people are those people who are below you in the same verticals. The notion is simple, and it is about time allocation. This can be relatable to many aspects of life, but you can really apply it however it fits correctly in your life, from your boss, peers, to your friends and your family. So how do we go about understanding it, well the notion is that you should be spending 33% of your time with people that are less skilled than you in a particular area, 33% of your time with people that are on your same level, and 33% of your time with people that are more skilled than you are.

The Same Class: Your Peers, your match which you look to outplay and skill.

Firstly, we must understand why this ratio is important? Let us start at square one, these are your peers and people that have a similar skill set as you. One really should want these to be around these people, the reason is simple you want the similar audience as yourself so that you can identify factors of how they are going to be growing with you, these are your supporters from the same performing audience, if you do well, you might get these people excited. Look back in your contact list and jot down a list of 3 people, one should be your colleague, one should be your friend and the last should be a dear one, and they are going to be very supportive when you help them with something. You are building your skillset together, so you are going to grow together.

When you are the senior

There is a lot to learn from this segment, an insight of how it is different now compared to when you were them. This segment of people is going to be looking to you for advice in a skill area and you are providing knowledge and advice. These people are the audience most likely open to learning from you, you reflect on your life endeavours to them. They are the new millennials, probably just entering the workforce, when you explain to them how investing has/hasn't worked for you because hands-on experience is the best teacher. a. Let us be honest, one does really take time to accept and make changes with difficulty, if we had known the outcomes ourselves, like we do after experiences, we would have given the same advice to ourselves. Examples could be not chase trends in investing and especially to not be deterred by noise in the market.

Why is this so important? Well once you can teach something to someone else, you really feel like you know it. I can remember struggling through geometry in school, it felt like Tom Cruise during any Mission Impossible movie. I finally got a hang of it, just as Tom Cruise got towards the end of the movie, I could groom the other juniors just like Tom Cruise groomed Simon Peg in spying. The reason is, I had more experience with the concepts by this point and my friends were looking to me to explain it to them because I had already been through it. That is when I really began to grow and by giving out advice and correcting peers younger than me my confidence level was boosted. Teaching someone a topic, makes it stronger for you. If you can identify before how to create passive income sources, one would not chase a high-paying job and be taxed the highest bracket. You could suggest them, to open a corporation where you can fulfil your passive income sources and aspirations, while being taxed at a lower rate.

The Third 33%: People you get to learn from and the MOST IMPORTANT SEGMENT

These are your idols, your seniors or even your boss. One should never ever stop learning from any source; a successful entrepreneur or a successful individual knows that there are many problems to solve, many experiences to learn from and who better than the ones who have done and achieved more than you, but also failed more than you.

This is arguably the hardest 33% to get access to. If you are an entrepreneur, this is the 33% that have already made it, but those people are so busy that they often do not have as much time to do the teaching anymore. For me as I mentioned I had 5 seniors who I looked up to, 3 to whom I had no access directly to. These gentlemen were Cristiano Ronaldo, Virat Kohli, Akshay Kumar, Grant Cardone and a senior partner in my firm. I used to summarise their teachings, they had multiple sources of income (also the richest), probably the hardest working in the industries. For me, the first 4 were Icons and inspirations, I am going to start with my personal favourite Cristiano Ronaldo, I am a huge Real Madrid Fan, so that goes to show my bias towards him. The known fact about him is that he's the best footballer in the world (arguably), as of 2019 he made close to 60 Million $ a year as salary, that goes to show he makes 75$ an hour or 5 million $ a month. But this was not his only source of earnings. Rather this is only approximately one-third of his yearly earnings, he typically earns another 70-80 million $ via endorsements of world renowned brands of Nike, Armani, Tag Heuer, Egyptian Steel, EA Sports, PokerStars and Castrol. The last component which not many know about are his business investments, he has a line of hotel chains, a clothing line and also his own steel company. Put together he makes another 60 million $ from these as well. He has used his 9-5 or his active income to create streams of passive income and has also allowed his fame to create multiple sources of income for him. Ronaldo's earnings were not fully affected, and he was on an island with his family for a month, still earning on his passive income sources He is an epitome of creating multiple sources of income, he does not really have to work to make more than 90% of his income and he did create all these sources of income as a millennial.

Next up, is India's favourite prince, the captain of the Indian Cricket Team, Virat Kohli, he is again arguably the best cricketer of this generation. He earns close to 1 million $ from the BCCI as cricket fees and another 2 million $ from his contract with Royal Bangalore Challengers, but this is not even a fourth of his yearly income, he is an active investor in start-ups, he is also the brand ambassador of Audi, Colgate-Palmolive, Google, Herbalife, New Era, Oakley, Puma, Tissot and Uber to name a few. Virat Kohli collectively represents twenty-two brands and when put into perspective with his fee for every endorsement, one can only imagine how big a contributor this is to his net worth. He was also on the top position of the Forbes Celebrity 100 list, thanks to his earnings of Rs 252 crores, as reported by Forbes. Moving on to his other vertical of income, Mr. Kohli investigates the different verticals of business he can tap into, with great awareness of the Virat Kohli brand. He transformed his jersey number into a brand – One8, there is a restaurant by his name in the Delhi Airport as well. The slightly aged investment in the hospitality industry came in the form of Nueva, a fine dine bar and restaurant. This one is also based in Delhi and has been in operation for more than 2 years now. Notably, One8 has a collaboration with Puma for a category of athleisure wear and shoes, and an energy drink by the name Ocean. Kohli is the part owner of a gym, established in 2015. New to his bouquet of investments, is the one with his wife and Bollywood superstar Anushka Sharma as they invested in an insurance start-up, which goes by the name of Digit. The way he has transformed himself into a brand and allowed himself to be a millennial raking in 40 million $ a year and only 7.5 % of that coming from cricket, shows how he leverages his brand and creates passive income sources. He creates more assets and allows himself to focus on his games, as a priority only if it delivers less than 10% of his yearly income. He spends time outside of his cricket, by sacrificing sufficient time of his leisure to grow his income by 10X.

My next idol and inspiration is Akshay Kumar, a rag to riches Bollywood star, he is fourth on Forbes highest paid actors list, he also makes 62 million $ a year. I was lucky enough to work with him on a venture, to witness greatness. He is someone, who arguably has the best work ethic, he does 4 movies in a year and has the perfect work-life balance by not working on Sundays and 6 weeks a year off. Sounds impossible? Let us dive into how he does this ? He charges 7.5 million $ a movie and allows only 90 days to shoot it, his terms, and his work ethic, allow him to deliver the same, with great excellence. For someone who starts of at 4:30 AM, Akshay Kumar maintains the ideology of not investing in different verticals apart from the film industry. A key take-away – He invests in himself first, in the Bollywood industry. The actor owns two production houses - Hari Om Entertainment and Grazing Goat Pictures. These production companies have financed not just 50-60% of his movies, but other movies as well. He reaps in two sources of income from the same vertical, one from acting i.e. being the highest paid actor in Bollywood, he also benefits hugely through his production houses. This is investing in a production line, which did not involve too much time to Mr. Kumar's personal balance sheet as an asset, this creates another source of income from the same job i.e. acting. Mr Kumar is hugely inspired by "RICH DAD POOR DAD" by Robert Kiyosaki. He personally has a huge portfolio of Real Estate; he owns houses and warehouses worldwide. He owns properties in Canada, Mauritius, and many in India. There is a lot to learn from him, about investing in yourself, your mediums of income to multiply them, the investments in work ethic i.e. how to fulfil 3 times of a normal Bollywood actor at probably double their age. He invented another source of income by the skill, experience, and excess cash he had. One does require these 3 attributes to become a sophisticated investor, even if the investment is in yourself.

Grant Cardone is known as a performance coach, sales guru, fund manager, but mostly known as a big time real estate investor. He believes in the philosophy of unlimited sources of income, he is a keynote speaker for many sales organisations. He believed in only creating assets, which will create sources of income via organisations at a lower taxed rate. He has many webinars and seminars regarding the work ethic to develop the extra sources of income, you can read up on 10X and Cardone Capital. Getting access of the top 33% bracket is not easy, but we must try to seek inspiration from them via digital mediums. This does not mean picking up news on their latest gossip, but rather following their interviews regarding their careers, focusing on their victories over failures, by constantly learning from their failures. But to be honest, while we would be inspired by these icons, real life learning would be from the seniors, who you can learn from in person.

Lastly, touching upon the ones whom I did have access to, who helped shape my perspective in a large way. The senior partner at my firm, managed major big-ticket client's financial assets, probably the youngest senior partner in the history of the firm, I know it sounds like an oxymoron, youngest and senior partner. He created e books, webinars and online courses on career advice, MBA programs and investment management. He in fact told me, over the last year he has grossed double of his salaried income. He had the experience and education, when the company went for an IPO, he used maybe 5 to 10 % of the money he got from the stake sale and invested in these cash cows. His own YouTube channel gets him 20000$ a month, that is the amount he made by investing 50000$ and the experience and education he had.

The senior partner would be the prime example for this learning. The best way is to have these people as your friends, but what if that has not happened yet? Reach out to them and ask them for coffee or whatever other medium of engagement, as simple as a phone call or let you sit on one of their meetings as a learner. You could build something productive for them, do free assignments for them, or just an admiration email describing how inspiring their work is. As long as they have time to read that email, I can assure you that they are going to be honoured and grateful that you put in the time and effort to write that email. They might even be willing to spend some time with you for that coffee meeting which you had pursued, or maybe if you're lucky enough and managed to touch their emotional side, they might even bring you on as an intern or learner.

How to overtake your peers during the journey towards financial freedom

Unlike your regular road journey, where overtaking while driving is frowned upon, I believe that these smart shortcuts in the journey towards financial freedom, will help you achieve financial freedom sooner. As the old saying goes, it is not the destination, it is the journey which counts. To be financially free, entitles you towards early retirement and not spending the average time a working individual spends in the rat race.

Goal Oriented investing, is undoubtedly the most important criteria for investment management, go back to the drawing board and write down your goals and reverse engineer to today to see how much investment is required. Keep a number in your mind, which is committed each fortnight or each month. A study demonstrated that the farther away a goal appears, the more doubtful, you seem to be about when it will happen, the more probable outcome is that you would give up. So in addition to focusing on big goals (a house, child's education and the most important retirement), keep a focus on your smaller and immediate goals along the way that will make faster results, it could be as minimum as saving before a holiday with loved ones, or buying a phone.

The next way to overtake is in fact not a frequent exercise, but a very rewarding one, one should learn when and how to negotiate their job or terms of engagement and it should not be limited to just salary discussion, which is undoubtedly important, but it should go beyond it . If you are letting go off your current job and pay, you need to know the obvious it is got to be higher. Getting a potential employer to name the figure first means you can then push them higher. The important part of your discussion, which goes beyond both the discussion of variable and fixed pay is your working hours, designations, study and paternity/maternity leave, travel time, and which assignments you'll be operate on, could all be things that a future employer or partner may be willing to discuss.

Learning how to budget is probably one of the most important focuses of successful millennials who have achieved financial freedom. This is the starting point of every other financial goal in life, if you have take-home pay of approximately 1500 $ a month, in what manner can you pay rent, food, insurance, health care, loan repayment and entertainment without running out of money. The budget must include all your essentials, a minor portion of your desires; the goal is to save for emergencies and tomorrow's aspirations. We live in a highly technology evolved world, direct debits is the way forward, so I suggest to automate as much as possible, so that the finances you've allotted for a specific goal or expense gets there with little or no effort on your end. A responsible partner or a support group can assist with that, so that you are held responsible for choices that could stir you away from the budget. My personal recommendation is not the popular 50/30/20 budget. The common plan is where you spend roughly 50% of your after-tax dollars on necessities, no more than 30% on wants, and at least 20% on savings and debt repayment. I opt for a very different budget style approach, for my after-tax income, I first invest in myself, be it courses, education, side hustles and investments, this helps build my potential and financial assets. This for me varies between 35-40% of my monthly budget. The next vertical of my budget, would be spent on essentials/needs which could include rent, groceries, electricity etc. This vertical constitutes of 25-30% of my monthly budget. The last vertical, would be for my entertainment, which would be for travelling, pleasures and luxuries. This gets the last priority in my spending budget because it is not going to add to my future assets. This budget forces me to take upside hustles to increase my disposable income. Initially this plan, would allow me to increase my luxuries, but what it did for me eventually, is it motivated to build my assets both financially and otherwise. When you save first for your future, you will be motivated to not enjoy luxuries on the remains. This emotional angle will help you decide if the luxury expenditure is truly necessary. This is perhaps the most important takeaway for growth in your journey towards financial freedom.

The biggest hurdle to overcome and move forward on the road to financial freedom, is reducing debt. If you have a heap of debt, some weight of the shoulder is released, when you start paying off the smaller liabilities, these baby steps are the ones that can give you the belief to handle and reduce the larger debts. If in dire need of funds, consider the use of loans, which will not cost you more than 25% of your monthly income. The other way to handle your budget better, is via keeping track of your expenses. The miscellaneous, the planned or the unplanned ones, which can create a hole in your pocket and throw you off track in your road to financial freedom. These are often the mediums where you get trapped in the same circles and do not seem to be making progress on your journey towards financial independence. We have to learn the art of evaluating expenditures by charge per use, it may seem more smarter on the wallet weight to buy a fashionable 5 $ T-shirt than a standard 50 $ T-shirt, if quality isn't your criteria and you are going to wear it maybe once or max twice. At the time of evaluating whether the latest technological product, gadget to ease your work in the kitchen, or apparel item is adding real meaning, take in account, how often you will use it or wear it. Buy experiences, not things, directing your money in the direction of expenses like a concert or an industrial visit, do not think of splurging it on costly material objects, will give you a better smile for your investment. There is very modern research to support that conclusion. It is effortless to fall into the trick of buying for the person people will accept you as, not who you truly are or should become. When you are thinking about saving, start saving right that day, not the week after. Do not wait for that next cheque or the next raise to come. DO not go on a reverse gear in your journey towards financial freedom, by pushing your saving agenda to the next year. Right this moment, as your reading this, start looking for an ETF fund. The best part about investing now, is that your get a bigger benefit from compounding in the future. That is the power of compounding, a year can make 5 % effect to your total net worth at 60. Falling prey to the habit of dipping into savings early will damage you several times over. For beginners, you are nullifying all the hard work you have done so far keeping money aside. You are preventing that money from growing at a compounding rate. Secondly, you will be punished for an early withdrawal, and those punishments are usually heavy financially setting you a few years back in the journey of financial freedom. Lastly, you will get hit with a tax bill for the funds you remove. All these aspects make redemption early on, should be a very last option.

Now, that we have figure a road map given the skills you need to develop, the network you need to create and the thought process towards personal finance you need to change. None of the mentioned mediums of change will take place, unless and until you decide mentally, what is the way forward. The change of one's mental attitude towards taking personal finance seriously is the major difference someone who's financially independent and someone who's not.

CHANGE YOUR MENTAL ATTITUDE TOWARDS PERSONAL FINANCE

Since mental attitude is a vaguely broad area, we are going to look at examples to exhibit how the correct mental attitude adds steps towards your journey towards financial freedom and how the incorrect attitude sets you back.

CAUTION- I will be breaking a few stereotypes for the same

"Money makes money"- No it does not, what it takes is you yourself. There are so many rags to riches stories out there, be it Jeff from AMAZON or Elon Musk from Tesla, who's company is now more valuable than Toyota, they didn't inherit any money, they worked day and night to increase their skills and capabilities, so that they could achieve financial independence. Now, ask your self did it take money from your end to act up on your skill set potential and develop potential passive income sources by using enormous amounts of capital, or did you just out hustle your peers by doing more than what they did by looking outside of a 9-5 commitment to working.

"Money does not grow on trees"- This is what you might have heard right from when you wanted something from your parents, maybe even in your pre-teen years. This could be something which the other kids got, but it was out of your parents' budget. This statement did not mean, it is not yours to have. What it meant, was figure out a way to earn enough on your own to buy it. In this process, I can guarantee you that, the real reason why you should or should not get that object will be clearer.

Amongst the people who are reading this book, there are few people who can assert that they have NOT ONCE missed a liability due date or never gave in to their short term gratifications and avoided long term financial growth, by going on an spur-of-the-moment over indulging session, and NOT ONCE invaded their savings for a luxury. If you are one of those individuals, you should perhaps be the next financial pundit. Whether or not you do this consistently or infrequently, consider self-forgiveness in overindulgence.

Forgiving yourself for the financial embarrassment you were or you are in right now is very important. If you do forgive yourself, it stops you from being a prisoner to your earlier self, hoping this book inspires you to make changes. If you dwell in your past, you do not give yourself the opportunity to grow. One has to learn to let go of what happened in the past, be it a bad business partner or a failed business model. You should now look to move your focus away from financial embarrassment, so that you can make space for healthier mental attitude towards money. It is imperative to recognize and acknowledge what expenditures lead to only short-term gratifications, while at the same time they force you to fall short of achieving your long-term goals. Many of us make several expenditures and income decisions in our lives, performing this for just a week and then assessing the outcomes for patterns can be as easy a process to strengthen your consciousness of your attitudes. When you have more clarity on your attitude, you can identify principles and behaviours that influence your ability to be focused on your goals and re-evaluate the future goals.

In the information age where there is currently a lot of social media present, it is much easier to get carried away by drawing comparisons. You and even I have compared ourselves to other people like friends, family, celebrities, and personalities. When you are doing this self-demeaning act, it is doing you no good to your mental attitude towards preparing for your financial freedom journey, use them as mere inspirations and motivations to bring out the best within you. You see someone wearing a Gucci T-shirt and you do not have one, most often you will feel bad for not having it and kicking yourself out of low self-esteem. That Gucci t-shirt is not a representative of wealth, you do not see Mark Zuckerberg, who is worth 60 billion $ wearing that also. A true display of wealth is not through luxuries, it is via assets. I once heard a very close friend and mentor of mine say to me "I'm not going to pay 1000 $ to wear some else's initials on my feet". On social media, everyone is rich and famous. Indeed, anybody using an Instagram or a Facebook, cannot help but observe that the individuals are projecting a classier version of their day to day activities. You will notice that there are individuals who also endorse their representations for high class standing, expensive hotels, first class flights, beautiful women (Dan Bilzerian visitors couldn't help but notice) manage to show individuals glowing (literally) happiness, or simply showing off their extravagant life. Stop comparing what you know about yourself to what you see of someone else (their projections of the best life). Moreover, you or even I do not understand the personal details of the individual whose post you saw on an Instagram or Facebook medium. That individuals or the group of individuals may appear to have a fabulous life filled with luxuries, but it could be driven by credit card debt or a bank loan! All that glitters is not gold. When you make comparisons and find yourself lacking, you are switching attention away from focused on your own financial goals to them. With the correct mental attitude, you would be mentally prepared to see your vision for the future and once you have determined your final goal and also clearly defined your road map. There is nothing more important than to reverse engineer and decide the first step to achieving that goal via your roadmap.

REVERSE ENGINEER TO SQUARE ONE

In today's information age, investing in any form of asset, has evolved greatly. The magnitude of investments has grown more than tenfold over the past few years. Investment is regarded as very personal and sacred. Today there are multiple options in automobiles i.e. cars, trucks, scooters etc, the same way there are multiple options in investments known as investment vehicles. There are asset classes, then there are sub-asset classes based on style and size. Just as every automobile vehicle has a different function, cars are for 4 passengers and trucks are for goods transport, the same applies for the investment vehicles. An investment product or vehicle takes you to your destination in terms of horizon and how bumpy the road is determined by your risk appetite. The vehicle takes you from where you are financially to where you want to be financially. Each vehicle has its purpose in the journey to the financial goal. Their purpose can be, but not limited to capital appreciation and income.

In today's time there are a lot of people who want to make quick money without a destination or a proper roadmap for that investment vehicle. This is called "trading". A person trading could be a speculator or an active investor with a short horizon, one typically must make much more than the supposed aim in returns, because of the higher short-term taxation impact of the same. Trading itself is a profession, it's different from investing, and the defining difference is the time period. A trade typically has a shorter time horizon. Apart from the usual equity, fixed income, real estate and private equity asset classes, more and more asset classes are been created every year. Too many people get attracted and stick to one kind of asset class, like stocks or just real asset, but fail to look at other asset classes, which could have a better risk-reward ratio. Diversification is the key to successful result-oriented performance.

When you are unclear on your financial plan or goal, all these asset class options will only further confuse you. If you want to be a legit good investor, you should get hung up on one type of asset rather come up with your future goal. The good investor sees the far ahead mission, reverse engineers to what is required of him or her today and then creates a road map to reach there. The questions you are to ask yourself as you embark on your journey to financial freedom, is which asset classes can you invest, what is the amount? is it systematic or lump sum? what is the risk-reward ratio? Reverse engineering to today, where you are in the first stage of investment, look at that goal with putting mainly the horizon into perspective. The analysis required from your end, is to investigate the average return required, keep some in liquid funds/ arbitrage for an emergency fund and then start investing today for the goal. The most important part of investment is the plan, do not invest until you have one. This is the most important part because a disciplined approach is the only way to reach your ultimate financial goal.

When you are formulating a plan, you need to be aware of major hurdles which will arise in your journey towards financial freedom, as this journey has many up's and down's. One certainly has to be driven to achieve their goals, but also has to be cautious, because this journey is like a snakes and ladder game. The snakes can set you back months and even years, if you're not cautious in your road to financial independence.

BE DRIVEN, BUT BE CAUTIOUS

Lesson – 101 - Do not hurt yourself financially during your journey towards financial freedom.

The widely famous perception is that money solves for all problems. Unfortunately, that statement is only half right, as it can be a solution to many problems, but not all. It can also create problems, in the last century, more people have gone from rich to bankrupt than from rich to richer. One of the major reasons for that is because of the way people use their old money habits to manage new money. When Mr. Y had started his own business in 2010, the business had grown to a large audience and during the early 2010's the dominant advertising mediums were television commercials, road hoardings and pamphlets used for promotion. The reason the business had grown, was because he was targeting the correct audience with the best possible technology at that point. Eventually as an industry, technology and customer base evolved, the business started seeing diminishing growth rates. What Mr. Y failed to notice is that the new potential customers are not going to come on board with the older technologies and business practices. He would have to upgrade the technology and also the marketing techniques, as the new customers are more internet savvy, they could be target via new marketing verticals, Mr. Y was not going to find new customers via television commercials, road hoardings and definitely not through door-to-door pamphlets advertising. Mr. Y went on to make a few more errors in multiple business verticals. He had to restart building wealth, but this time with experience. It set him back at least 10 years and that is a decent amount of time lapse in anyone's career, because his business was stuck to older ways of operating and not adapting. The reason his business failed was because of lack

of reworking on his new audience potential and. This highlights one out the many failure verticals one can face in the new age social media audience. As an individual, your skills, marketing and knowledge base has to evolve, as it's imperative to stay in trend to survive and grow.

Individually I take inspiration from my favourite childhood game, Snakes and Ladder. There are snakes, which will set you back and there are ladders which will help you reach closer towards financial freedom. Another type of failure, which is not professional, but is more personal is when an individual ends up buying more liabilities when you get the first wave of wealth.

There are ways where you can avoid the snake trap, which can lengthen your age of financial freedom.

- Emotional spending- The secret to failure of many people who have become rich quick, but also have then become bankrupt. When a significant amount of money hits their bank accounts, there is this sudden euphoria of intelligence, which seems to have emerged within themselves, but it is the emergence of stupidity. A very close friend of mine, a chartered accountant, he mentions that whenever anyone gets rich, they buy luxuries, which add no value and create debt. He said they buy luxury cars, upgrade their wardrobe, go on unnecessary trips and various other luxuries. They have not just spent off potential of creating new assets, they have created another form of liability.

- "I am now a High Net Worth Individual (HNI)"- This is an aspect which finally makes many people a "Socially Acceptable Individual". When suddenly someone gets rich either through inheritance or hard work, a sense of sudden intelligence arises, it gives many people a false sense of intellect. In fact, what it creates, is an ego self-defensive vibe. We are in the social media age today, where we meet or see profiles of individuals who don't know the I of investing, with headlines on their LinkedIn profiles like "SERIAL investor/entrepreneur" or "HNI", the definition of a HNI, comes from reaching a certain amount of wealth or a certain amount of annual income, this varies from country to country. A sudden infusion of wealth does not grow an individual's financial intelligent quotient, you need actual financial literacy to keep the financial IQ in play. Another delusional title and investment, which is a wealth sinker is investing in start-ups where an individual has zero or less knowledge about the business model and customer base, but he is just in a hurry to join the boat, which will only sink that individual financially. The first point talks about personally buying debt, here when investments without knowledge, skills, education or even experience in the field are putting a lot of money at risk, because the odds of success are low, 99% of start-ups fail. An individual should only invest in assets, which will create assets in the future or invest in educating himself or herself. One should look to gain experience and exposure, or work with someone who does have knowledge, experience, education, and skills in that business vertical. Never work alone, always work in a team.

- The "new money"- This is something I have learned been brought up in India. Not many people who suddenly are rich, due to hard work, luck, or inheritance, often get richer or keep that money safe. The one's who do become richer or witness some capital appreciation, are those who have prepared with money-management skills, quoting Warren Buffet again, "If you can't manage 10000 dollars, you won't be able to manage a million dollars". One seriously must change their money-management skills to prevent losing the fortune you might have inherited or worked for. There are patterns to break, both emotionally and financially. If there are thousand ways to make money, there are million ways to spend that money.

- The art of saying "no"- This is something most parents teach their children, my father always told me, it is always easy to say "yes" to self-indulging and very difficult to say "no" to it. He enforced so many objections against many expenditures, which were just hard work down the drain. The reason I can relate to this, is with experience, some luxuries which I was stubborn to indulge in as a teenager are of no value today. This also brings me to another point I would like to highlight, is investing with love. Emotional investing is investing with family, friends, and other loved ones. An important aspect of staying rich is saying no to your loved ones and yourself most of the times, when it comes to short term gratification or investment in ventures only out of love. As seen in point 1, the debt piled on can inhibit personal financial freedom. The loved ones can be your investee if you allow proper due diligence as an investor, not as a loved one. There is also something seemingly interesting about having wealth, the banks often lend more to people who have more money, it is a debt trap. This makes one think the current wealth can be used as collateral to pursue, a so-called optimistic venture, investment or even a speculation. This will be a gamble, so best to avoid banks, when you have access to money.

- The Mentality - A poor individual or a lower to middle class individual who has recently gained excess cash in abundance, will have the mental trait of their earlier mental trait. They are so afraid of losing what has taken a decent amount of time to accomplish, that they don't look to grow more than that, they create a mental ceiling or a cap to where their wealth will grow. The fear of being poor increases at the time of wealth abundance.

- Time Wasters – A lot of people spend more time procrastinating about a hiccup than actually spend time solving the problem. We as individuals like to please others, so we don't really get into the habit of saying no. We know or are individuals who spend too much time "hanging out" or "Netflix", rather than using that time as a tool to grow further. The most dangerous time waster is social media addiction, an average millennial spends about 3 hours a day on social media, which often leads to procrastination, as it is showing you the good part of life. This addiction often leads you to forego existing timelines and goal aspirations, it's more addictive than cigarettes, as 75% of the millennials open their social media screens the minute they wake up.

The reason why most people do not grow further in their financial freedom or do not move ahead on the journey towards complete financial freedom, is because they stop. The path to financial independence, is a road which can only grow and grow. There are two aspects of financial freedom, one is the road to wealth, the other is the road to grow that wealth. Financial independence is not a lottery ticket won, it is fuelled with financial literacy which requires financial education and high financial intelligence quotient. The other reasons, why people go to zero after touching 100 for a few months/years is because they have no tracking of their expenditures, be it at a personal or their corporate level. A part of the financial education also includes studying expenses of the rich or the expenses of successful corporates. There are some expenses, which are assets, and some are not. You should be able to identify the good apples from the bad. From experience, when I sold a particular venture, I got access to some money, I opened a MBA fund, registered for CFA courses, bought a laptop, suits, a car, a television set, a trip to 3 foreign destinations, a personal trainer, a language class and saved the remaining 40% in growth paper assets like large cap and small cap stocks. A small exercise, to see where you are with your financial education, identify the good from the bad from my purchases. Remember not all of the wealth created, has to be created towards liabilities, there is only one life and only one millennial age span before I become old, to manage what I can do young and what I cannot do.

There was a balance in between the luxuries i.e. cars, trips, and assets i.e. others. Yes, you should build assets and create more income, but you should not avoid the simple joys, be it the luxury of a trip and a four-wheeler. But today I learnt about new business markets in my trip and the car helps me reach my meetings faster. A fitness trainer is an investment in my health, because one can only achieve wealth if they have a good emotional quotient, and a session in the morning allows me to push myself all throughout the day. A language class helped me build a larger customer base. An MBA will help me grow my knowledge and skills; a CFA charter will help fine tune these kills. The best investment every young millennial can make is in their suits and other aspects of appearance and dressing. People do take you seriously, if your formally or properly dressed. Individuals tend to lose interest in your work. if you are not formally dressed. Believe me, you really do not feel like working with someone, if they are dressed in T shirt and jeans on a Monday, why would you expect their perception to be somewhat else.

Every individual no matter how cautious you are, is bound to fail at some level, being driven and cautious at the same time, will reduce the odds of failure, but unfortunately it cannot eliminate it completely. An individual learns more in the small and big failures in life, than any individual learns in success.

EVERY FAILURE IS A STEP CLOSER TO SUCCESS

TRY AND TRY, UNTIL YOU SUCCEED

Every single person in life is always in a race to do achieve all professional and personal milestones, to get good grades, to get a good job, to be the best at finishing first. Jack Ma has an interesting quote on this, he says "If one should not aim to be at the top 10 of the class or top 10 in the logging hours game in the corporate world". Just to clarify, he also does not say that he wants you to be in the bottom 10. The wealthy individuals of an investor mentality are usually in the middle batch. The reason he comes out with this unique opinion is, the mid-performers have the time to pick up skills and proceed with side hustling. Getting a high paying job and aiming to top your batch, does not come with the flexibility to pursue passions and skills. Jack Ma's Harvard applications have made it to major motivation pages on literally every medium. How he failed to get in, and how that failure led him to eventually start ALIBABA, and today be a retired billionaire.

For representative purposes, let's embark on a journey of two opposing personalities. For simplicity sake, we are going to label them A and B, these two have been very influential to my position on the road to financial freedom. Mr. A is currently someone who was a top achiever in school and goes to study a post graduate program, his belief was that success comes from education, which will get him the best job and probably high-paying. Mr. B was the mid-achiever in college, as he was always reading books on culture, industries, economies, and many other verticals. His main aim was to be rich, but not via only a job. He knew a 9-5 would only give him a standard of living which is comfortable in the long run, since the tax rates for income are probably the highest, cutting your disposable income to probably two-thirds. He would still work in the job, since he is not from a rich family, but what he would do to fuel his passive income sources with his active income was intriguing, motivating and enlightening at the same time. Mr. B was someone who always believed failure is the best teacher, he would rather pursue something where he fails repetitively and that would teach him from experience. His endeavours have helped him understand what he knows both what should be done and what should not be done to achieve success. Mr. B was someone who always pursued passive endeavours, he would be encouraging the mistakes, instead of accepting them as it is, he believed in challenging himself to learn and grow not only in skills, but also experience. If your starting your journey you should have more traits on Mr. B, as these traits allows a better learning and growing experience.

This chapter does consist of a lot of inspirations of how failures lead to success. The ex-richest man in the world, Warren Buffet, also came from the same ideology that failure gives birth to success. No successful man has reached where he/she is or has been without failing and learning from the mistakes which led to the failures. He tried investing in a clothing line which was in a distressed security category. His idea was to pursue changing the internal organization and framework of the company, to make it a success. But he failed, for many reasons, first he was not from the apparel industry, secondly it was beyond repair, it was attractive in pricing only because of the discount. He also failed as textile manufacturing in North America was well past its prime and moving to emerging countries, because of the cheap labour and cheap raw materials. This clothing line was called Berkshire. Today Berkshire Hathaway, will probably ring a bell for being one of the biggest shares in the American Stock Exchange. This failure, had two important lessons from it, firstly was the real estate he acquired for a throw away price, which he learned to have great value because of the location and also the Berkshire which was acquired to change the textile industry (only later to realise as a decline industry) was where he started buying company shares to become the richest investor in the world.

Elon Musk, the hugely controversial billionaire, had his own share of failures which led to his success of today. It is quite impressive, right from getting kicked out of this seminal role in PayPal in the midst of his honeymoon to his 3 major failures in launching the space rockets and even inclusive of his numerous failed attempts at launching Tesla. Today, Tesla is almost at par (2019-2020 valuation) with General Motors, a company which is known as the pioneer of the automobile industry and existing for more than half a century. He believed that if we are not encountering obstacles, then nothing new is created. He accepted his failure of not acknowledging that his vision during his failures were highly optimism driven endeavours. He tried many ventures, sold some of them, failed in most of them. He was doing this both full-time and post his 9-5 job. His work ethic was the strongest in quantity, clocking in 80-90 hours a week. He did so much more, than others, one of the reasons of his net worth and financial independence.

Today he is worth 60 Billion $, because he failed too many times so as to inadvertently eventually succeed.

Another example of failure was LEVIS STRAUSS, he was someone who had decided to make a discovery and a disruption in the field of mining. He later realised, he lacked training and knowledge of mining, having locked himself out trying to continuously pursue mining. Levis lost and almost tore all his clothes, because of the mining hard work exposure he was encountering. He realised due to the heat and low level digging involved in mining, he could manage shirtless, but could not risk not wearing pants, he used to sew clothes every night for the miners. This is how a multibillion-dollar brand was created. The name Thomas Edison, if history were your favourite subject in school, like it was for me, would ring a bell. In case not, let me just start with- he was the one who invented the light bulb. Thomas would have never founded the light bulb, if he were the employee of the company he ultimately founded, today known as General Atlantic.

What differentiates these individuals from the others who have not seen such success yet in their careers, is the mental attitude. Every single human, hates making mistakes, but what reflects to investing in yourself better, is learning from your mistakes. If you are looking to build passive income streams, your first podcast, your first YouTube Channel, your first blog, your first business, your first attempt at Harvard, it is not necessarily going to be a success. You will know if you truly deserve it, if you constantly pursue it, like MICHEAL JORDAN says, he failed 10,000 times in getting the ball in the hoop. Dwayne Johnson, failed as a football player, after hitting prime and questioned himself if it was right leaving WWE at his prime, after his first 5 movies were not commercial successes. I was not someone who was academically gifted, I only studied because I had to. I was always looking to learn outside, I often chased short term gratifications (luxury items), instead of investing in long term assets. What I mean, by long term assets, is paying yourself first, building an assets column in your personal balance sheet. I wish I was investing in the kind of assets, that will bring income later in life, instead of wasting the major part of my 20s, if I had created boundaries for myself of what I could achieve, and not worked on developing my skillset to improve upon what all I couldn't achieve, I would not have been able to build passive streams of income.

There are so many ventures I am still pursuing, you might even know how many attempts to get that prestigious charter I am still pursuing, I failed 5 times in each of my ventures and in exams. I created a CFO platform, to help celebrities get their clothing lines funded, I helped people get pitch ready, I tried selling sponsorship for celebrity cricket, I even failed at selling movies. Today I have built an active income and 2 major sources of passive income, only after being a failure in isolating myself losing friends and time with family, to pursue endeavours I was not skilled enough to manage. But today, I actively manage clients' money in the public market, because I spent half a decade in working on my skillset and even did it for free during my initial phases to gain clients, to now managing over 40 million $ in the Indian Capital Market. It was constant failures and learning from them, which enabled me to work on myself to reach my current potential. Each time, I failed I was dejected, I am human after all, but always found my lesson in reflecting and pushed myself towards success. Soon with failure, I was responding positively and trying on new sources of income or skillset to create new sources of income. I even tried my hand in the movie distribution business, where I was distributing records for B2B, it was a venture where I did not have the skillset or knowledge, all I had was the network. When I failed miserably in this, it is so contradicting to what I believe today, because I do not see myself in that field, to think back at it was probably the worst venture fit for me. But in all this, I developed a business connection, who is today my largest client in the wealth management business, since my first step into wealth management in 2014, and has stuck with me not only because of the business relationship we had created, but also because of the performance in his financial assets portfolio I was able to deliver, because of my improved skillset and a decent understanding of the Indian Equity Markets. What I learnt over this time, was that in school, you were given a lesson and then a test, but in

life you often are given a test and a lesson to learn back from it. Going back to Exhibit A, I consider him a big failure in life, because his play it safe attitude, led him to not have a job today at the age of 40. This happened, because he played it safe, he still looks to get a job by going for interviews and pursue what every highly trained in one skill labour does. That is focus on job security and not wealth creation. A famous man, said take care of your passive income as your working too hard for a company, who can replace you a week after you drop dead.

I can help you identify these people, who you might call peers, friends or even relatives. This can be a fun exercise, as if your building a better future, by working on building your passive income sources, you're going to let these people go from your life, as these people are toxic. First up are people who don't leave an opportunity to blame another person or an incident, which was never in their control or was supposed to help in the outcome. The next set of people are those that deny participation in the input when the output was failure but would have taken ownership if it was a success. The most dangerous lot of these, are those who lie about hard work. These are the most toxic people. The other two types of people are equally toxic, justifiers and quitters, the former is inclusive of people who justify failure with reasoning which is biased and isolating the person from all failures. The latter, who can be lazy at many times are those people who quit mid process and can influence you also to quit.

You might have heard this saying, you are the product of the people who you spend your most time with, so choose wisely. Risks, mistakes, and failures are important parts of human development, so one should learn to manage risks, instead of choosing to be an escape artist. Another human development is overcome emotional investing, be it in the stock market or in pursuit of a highly ambitious but unjustified endeavour.

I still work on side hustles, skillset improvement and pursuing the charter and might later consider an ONLINE MBA. Since we are in the COVID-19 phase, travelling for an MBA looks out of bounds at least temporarily. I want to grow myself by investing in myself to manage more money efficiently and help my clients grow their portfolios. Today's pandemic (COVID-19), has emerged as the greatest collapse in physical transactions, these are times when you revaluate your strategy, as good companies are available at huge discounts. We need to take this an opportunity and grow from the discounts available in the stock exchange. The discounts are not just limited to investing in the stock market, these are times when your expenditure on your "wants" will drop significantly. The opportunity provided is forcing you to give up short term gratifications, not because you can't afford them, is because you cannot access them. If you want to shop online, go to a bar, buy luxury items and the most important cut in expenses would be in travelling, use that money to invest in yourself, as you are your best investments.

COVID INVESTING

This is something not just every millennial, but I believe everyone reading this book can relate to. After the great depression in the early years of the 20th century and then the 2008 banking crisis, the COVID-19's impact has created a global slowdown. International trade (exports and imports) is expected to fall by between 13% and 32% in 2020 as the COVID 19 pandemic upsets standard economic activity and functioning of life across the globe.

The widespread range of outcomes for the projected decline is explained by the extraordinary nature of this global life crisis and the uncertainty around its exact impact on the company. Several economists believe that this failure will likely surpass the global economic trade slump brought on by the global banking crisis of 2008-09. The present approximations of the expected recovery in the following year, are also uncertain, with consequences depending largely on how long the outbreak persists and the effectiveness of the policy responses. "This crisis is first and foremost a health crisis which has forced governments to take unprecedented measures to protect people's lives," WTO Director-General Roberto Azevêdo said.

"The unavoidable declines in trade and output will have painful consequences for households and businesses, on top of the human suffering caused by the disease itself." "The immediate goal is to bring the pandemic under control and mitigate the economic damage to people, companies and countries. But policymakers must start planning for the aftermath of the pandemic," he said. "These numbers are ugly – there is no getting around that"

But a rapid, vigorous rebound is possible. Decisions taken now will determine the future shape of the recovery and global growth prospects. We need to lay the foundations for a strong, sustained and socially inclusive recovery. Trade will be an important growth vertical, along with fiscal and monetary policy. Keeping markets open and predictable, as well as fostering a more generally favourable business environment will be critical to spur the renewed investment we will need. If countries manage to work together, we will see a much faster recovery than if each country acts alone." The economic shock of the COVID-19 pandemic inevitably invites evaluations and comparisons to the global financial crisis of 2008-09. Both the COVID-19 and Global Financial crises are similar in a few contexts, but also very different that others at the same time. During the global financial crisis in late 2008 and during the COVID-19 economic crisis, some governments have again mediated with monetary and fiscal policy to fight against the recessions and provide financial support to businesses, employees, unemployed households and also unprivileged citizens. There are restrictions on traveling and maintaining distances from others to lower the magnitude of the spread of the virus, this limits the labour supply and movement, which are not correlated to ways the economies has responded to the 2008-2009 financial crisis. There are full sectors of national economies have been completely shut down, including hotels, restaurants, non-essential retail trade, tourism, and significant verticals of manufacturing.

The deflationary jolt from COVID-19 imposed global economic shutdowns; this is the strongest impact since the 1930s. Central banks were already failing and not being able to hit their inflation targets even before the impact of COVID-19 emerged. As of May 2020, the COVID-19, has led to economies to have an even bigger ditch to climb out of. We would require a large infusion of cash flow for years to grow up to that of Pre-COVID levels. This high amount of liquidity in combination with high government spending could provide support measures to assets and offers the potential for an economic recovery. The outlines of the post-coronavirus investment landscape will be shaped by many factors. I personally believe this provides an opportunity for investors, if you follow my earlier mentioned filters and take into consideration the longer-term vision and business cycle performances of businesses, this can be an opportunity to earn that extra return from the recent discount available in the market. I had mentioned how extra spending on liabilities will not bring wealth and income to your life. This period of quarantine, is the perfect time to work on improving your skillset, starting your side hustles, investing in stocks when everyone is selling in panic, because you know deep down, there is still an upside potential and all this is just noise. I prefer equities relative to fixed income; prefer large capitalization companies relative to smaller capitalization companies and over fixed income. I favour investment-grade bonds, which are of high quality and secure. You should buy on weaknesses and dips, as these price offerings are once in a lifetime opportunity.

When we look at post COVID investing, we should remember confidence is important virtue to have or strengthen further, it's a common trait to possess even when one was investing after the Great Depression or the banking collapse in 2008-2009. When we look at economies like Europe and USA, they have been built over a few hundred years, whereas India and Chinese economies and societies have been built over thousands of years. These are not going to break or be wipe out for a pandemic which lasts only for a few months. Only when a country's fundamental pillars are broke, does the company have a seriously permanent damage (5 years plus). The solution would come from reducing the disparity of income of the rich from the poor. All employees would have to

consider raising the pay, to bring the lower working class a standard of living of basic measure. The lower-class people form the base of the economic pyramid. On the day, this book goes for publishing, 13th May 2020, the Prime Minister of India, announced a large stimulus package, where the priority was shared between lower class people and unemployed people. Food would be provided to lower class citizens who have lost jobs. Through the initiatives taken by the government, cash is reaching accounts of people, who are benefitting from the "Direct Benefit Scheme". The tax refunds up to a point, were expedited and credited to business's and household's income.

If you are privileged enough to be financially literate and still have cash flows coming in at a time, when many firms are shutting shop, you should be grateful. There are many measures taken by the government, which will create limitations in productivity for the next year. One should start studying the basic benchmarks, not getting into the various different verticals impacted, just the basic benchmarks, like the large cap, mid cap and small cap in the size classification and sector-wise (any three preferences) for demonstrative purposes, we will start with telecom sector, pharma sector and discretionary goods. The indices study must have a 5-year horizon, possibly the day before lockdown, should be considered as the last day and then reverse engineered for 5 years, to note the growth before the COVID-19 impact. To illustrate my perspective better, as an exercise, I would urge you to do the same. The second part of this phase would also require noting the highest and lowest index value. This fifteen-minute exercise will explain both the peaks and the average returns of the same and illustrate a pattern for opportunity investing. So, after spending a sufficient time on these exercises, you have a bunch of numbers. The analysis you have done, allows you to know the growth potential of the stock, be it by noise, fundamental strengths or technical volume, the reasons for the high price could be overvaluation or undervaluation, one doesn't really know. This same is applicable for the lowest price of the stock over 5 years.

We now start with an average price of the 5-year cycle, for each of those preferences. This is my investing logic, for knowing one element of intrinsic value. This is a starting point for your investments, the number you get say for instance, 1000 Rupees. This value would most likely be at a discount today, because of the pandemic we are currently witnessing. An average decline, large cap representative benchmark in India is down 30%, so for understanding perspective, it is

700 rupees. If you are a first-time investor, who has done the research with the exercise mentioned about sector views or even geographic views, you are in luck. The effect of this pandemic has allowed you to purchase quality businesses at great discounts, you are not going to recognize gains in all your stocks. If your still not sure or afraid of the outcome, which is very natural. I would recommend you follow, Warren Buffet's investment style and probably the best investment for any new beginner at any time. The investment strategy, you would want to opt is a low-cost ETF (Exchange Traded Fund), where you would be replicating the 30 % current decline in the largest capitalisation benchmark. This could allow you to both gain on the upside and make money from economic recovery. There is a golden opportunity, more like a sale, but instead of sales in shopping malls which are liabilities and probably going to zero value from the time picked up of the shelf, these opportunities are assets, which will grow in value and add to your other source of income, known as paper (portfolio income). There is a couple of things to be aware about this investment style, it is not a one-time investment rather it is a systematically placed investment vehicle. With at least the current situation where the vaccine for COVID-19, has not been found to be deployed for the recovery of the infected and protection of others. There will be some volatility, so the investment frequency for instance could be invested weekly, fortnightly, or even monthly. This could vary based on your liquidity, though it is a bad time where job opportunities have been significantly reduced in sectors, if not eliminated. There are many people or most people, who have surplus money because of the lockdown, where you are not really spending. This could be the best time to save higher, write an e book, invest in another side hustle, read self-finance books, and invest in yourself. When you are investing in yourself, your allowing yourself to grow more to pay yourself first. You as an asset, should create more financial assets, to be protected and grow financially at the same time.

CONCLUSION

The reason I believe my experience can be fruitful for every millennial starting their journey towards financial freedom, is because I have seen more downs than ups in my personal journey. There is a lot of experience, good and bad I have had since the 10 years of embarkment on my journey toward financial freedom. Back in 2010, I had just started off with close to 10000$ in debt, it took me 2 years from that to finally eliminate debt.

Why, so much time? I made many wasteful expenditures which I thought would bring down my debt, by creating assets, but I was in fact accumulating more liabilities.

All over the world, a savings account majorly gives you a low interest rate, unless it was the purpose of an emergency fund or a short-term need, I did not really look at savings account. I often chose to invest my time and money, in building assets. For me it was a lot of investment in skill building and stocks initially. This gives me a good return on my finances and my happiness. I spend time and money building my content on my e- commerce platform, gaining more clients for my franchise and growing in my active income space (job), then actually running bank to bank finding the best interest rate on my savings account. I prefer to rent, rather than buy real estate, because in Mumbai where I am from, real estate is freakishly expensive. I am considering buying a home and setting aside funds (invested) to buy my own place in 10 years. One great mistake I avoided, was not being too starry eyed about owning an apartment in an up-market neighbourhood, not that I could not afford it, Indian Real Estate was giving a negative yield at that time. My credit card spending is limited to fuel, eating out and travelling intercity or globally, because of the cashbacks. I understand the reason, why someone would say "Do not get a credit card ", but I follow a strict principal of not spending that amount if I don't have it in my bank account, and the purpose is only cash back. The basic rule I follow is save more than spending, every month. But just do not save it, invest it. I personally invest in ETF's and the model described in the chapter "My investment philosophy".

I follow the "5" philosophy. If something or someone does not matter in the next 5 years, rest assured I would not divulge more than 5 minutes on it. I personally am a long term investor, I believe if I read every day for 5 years and don't touch my investments for 5 years, I will see results in my own investment (via reading) and stocks/business. I also have a philosophy, regarding categorization, if I categorize a purchase as a luxury, I do not purchase it unless I can buy it 3 times over. This itself has saved me a ton of money.

If you have just started investing or going to start investing (hopefully, after reading this book) it can initially overwhelm you. The reason this book is majorly for millennials, is because one should invest when they are young to see the power of compounding, before you and your family grow further. Let's say you're able to invest close to 75$ a week for the next 30-35 years, at a 10-12 % return, you would have more than a million $ at retirement, compared to just saving them in a locker or under your pillow, you would have close to 150000$ only.

I hope, this book can share insights how financial know-hows can be used to solve life's common problem, be money is the biggest problem solver in this world. Financial education is not taught in many universities, it is not a subject in ivy leagues, yet it is the most important lesson life can teach us. You should really start now, buy a book on personal finance, watch a millennial youtuber's finance experience, or attend a seminar. Start small, buy an index fund, invest in a stock, increase your skill. One thing I learnt because of COVID-19, is self-education is more important than college education. Work today on your side hustles, build your passive income. I personally manage all my expenses from my passive income and use my active income to build assets.

We all have the same amount of time in a day, we each get at least a dollar as an income in life, how we use it determines whether our children eat well or not in the future.

www.ingramcontent.com/pod-product-compliance
Lightning Source LLC
Chambersburg PA
CBHW071148240526
45465CB00024BA/2025